Self Esteem for Men

Boost your confidence and social skills, overcome low self-esteem, and transform into a fearless Alpha Male while eliminating insecurity, depression, and social anxiety.

Christian Ford

All Rights Reserved.

TABLE OF CONTENTS

INTRODUCTION 1

CHAPTER ONE : THE PRINCIPLES OF SELF-ESTEEM 3

CHAPTER TWO : SELF-ACCEPTANCE; A PATHWAY TO CULTIVATING HIGH SELF-ESTEEM 11

CHAPTER THREE : HOW TO LIVE PURPOSEFULLY 17

CHAPTER FOUR : GETTING RID OF HAPPINESS ANXIETIES 26

CHAPTER FIVE : BEING CONSCIOUS OF SELF 37

CHAPTER SIX : USING THE MIND AS A FORCE FIELD 46

CHAPTER SEVEN: YOU ARE ENOUGH! 56

CHAPTER EIGHT : WINNING THE WAR WITHIN 65

CHAPTER NINE : BEING RESPONSIBLE TOWARD REALITY 74

CHAPTER TEN : A COMMITMENT TO LEARNING ALWAYS 82

CHAPTER ELEVEN: KICKING ADDICTIONS OUT 91

CHAPTER TWELVE : HOW DO YOU TREAT OTHERS? 100

CHAPTER THIRTEEN : HUMILITY IS A TOOL 109

CHAPTER FOURTEEN : FALLING IN LOVE WITH YOURSELF 119

CHAPTER FIFTEEN : THE ART OF SUSTAINING SELF-ESTEEM 129

CONCLUSION 140

Introduction

There is a connection between the individual and success in every area of life. There is an aspect of life that must be developed for a person to reach their highest potential. In this book, you will discover what this concept is about and how it can be utilised to shape your world.

From the title, you know we are talking about self-esteem. The cat is out of the bag now, so we might as well get right to it, shall we? Every man desires freedom; it explains why most wars fought in times past were about gaining liberty.

However, freedom is only attained first within and then in the external sense. Self-esteem is about being free enough to embrace all of you and still being in love with your own character. The idea of self-worth is essential to every man's growth in life. Hence the reason you must take all you learn in this book seriously.

The objective of this book is on the cover page; you will read tips on how to boost your confidence level, fight off low self-esteem, and live a depression-free life.

This material is divided into several chapters that are interwoven. The sections are structured in such a way that if you succeed with one tip, you will most likely do the same with the others. The objectives we have shared are achievable if you stick to everything you learn here.

Think about this book like a journey you have embarked on with a friend who is quite knowledgeable. Therefore, as a friend, I will advise you to grab a glass of your favourite drink, sit on the most comfortable couch you've got, and enjoy the ride. By the end of this book, you will learn how to become more knowledgeable, bold, fearless, and daring.

Your journey to becoming an Alpha Male begins with the first chapter on the principles of self-esteem. Take pleasure in reading, learning, and growing.

Chapter One

The Principles of Self—Esteem

I had never met Matthew in person until one rainy Wednesday afternoon when he walked into my office looking dejected. Matthew had called earlier to schedule a meeting - and from the expression on his face, I could tell he had a lot on his mind.

Matthew worked as a data analyst for a tech firm and felt like he had not done enough nor achieved anything tangible in all his years of work. Matthew found it very difficult to express himself at all times, and at some point, other people had begun to think it was a mental issue.

After spending time together, we discovered that Matthew's inability to follow through with anything was actually due to low self-esteem. Matthew had lived his whole life thinking there was someone else out there who was better than him.

Self-esteem is a critical aspect of life because it affects everything a person does or believes. Self-confidence is the feeling of satisfaction a man has about himself, knowing that he is not perfect but is good enough for the world. This is the feeling of respect, trust, and faith in one's abilities and judgement.

There is high and low self-esteem.

When a person has very high self-esteem, it means he has come to a place of complete acceptance of who he is and has managed to build a feeling of self-worth that cannot be tarnished.

On the other hand, a person with very low self-esteem struggles with feelings of self-worth, acceptance of self, and to believe in his ability to build great relationships with others. So, you either have a high self-esteem or a low one. If it is the former, you are in a good place; but if it is the latter, this book was written to guide you into making your life better.

Before we get to the sections that provide solutions, you must first understand why one can have either high or low self-esteem. No one is born with low self-esteem. Just like anything else, it is acquired through habit, relationships with others, and the situations a person is exposed to regularly.

Just the same, no one is born with high self-esteem.

All men are made the same way, but the feelings they develop about themselves later in life stem from their experiences as children, teenagers, and adults.

In a bid to create excellent material on self-esteem, I had the privilege of interacting with people like Matthew, because I wanted to discover the root of the problem

Even if a person doesn't know that he has low self-esteem, from the moment the discovery is made, changes can begin. We have succeeded in considering two fundamental aspects thus far; firstly, that no one is born with high self-esteem, and secondly, that you can change how you feel about yourself.

You know some of the basic ideas. The next step is for you to become familiar with some of the principles of self-esteem.

The principles of self-esteem refer to some of the ideas that guide a person to become comfortable with himself. This is the first step to building self-esteem; you must be satisfied with who you are.

So what are the principles of self-esteem?

1. Visualization

The first principle of self-worth and building self-esteem is to visualize what you want your life to be. When you discover what you are unhappy about and how you feel about yourself, instead of fussing about it, take time off every day to visualize yourself the way you want to be.

What do you see as your characteristics? What kind of person do you want to become? In your mind, replace the negatives with positives and start to live out the authentic self-esteem experience you see in your mind.

2. Quiet Acceptance

This principle refers to the way you accept yourself for who you are. Oftentimes, we observe others and try to be like them. When we are consumed with the idea of being like someone else (often someone that we don't even know), we start to lose ourselves.

Quiet acceptance means you are aware of your flaws, you are in touch with your feelings, and you still accept yourself, regardless. This sense of satisfaction with oneself births ideas on how to become better; embrace all of you today!

3. Patience with Self

I have seen cases of people who started on this journey to better self-esteem and didn't see it through to the end because they weren't patient enough. It took you time to get here so it will also take you time to detox.

So, make up your mind not to give up on yourself today. Stick to all of the steps and tips, work on yourself continuously, and build a tough skin that can withstand the challenges you face. For you to have enough self-esteem to be patient with others, you must first be patient with yourself.

4. Self-Protection

As you become more patient with yourself, also remember to protect yourself from negativity. The most peculiar cases of low self-esteem often stem from an inability to control negative vibes.

You should protect yourself from thoughts, ideas, and feelings that are not consistent with what you want or desire for yourself. You need to kick out whatever is not compatible with a positive mindset and then replace it with something good.

Self-protection should be taken seriously because whatever thoughts you feed your mind over time will manifest in your life and cause healing or damage.

5. Happiness over Anxiety

This is a choice you must make daily; am I going to be happy or anxious? You make this choice daily through the little decisions you make. It is proven that some of the most fortunate people on the planet have very high self-esteem.

Anxiety, on the other hand, makes you feel uncomfortable; it causes you to become irritable and angry over things you cannot control. Being anxious will never work for someone who wants to experience changes within himself.

Make up your mind today to be happy!

6. The Power of Words

An essential principle for you to stick to is the power of words. On this quest toward better self-esteem, you will have to use affirmations to get the results you desire.

Say those lovely things you want to see manifest in your life and watch them become truth. If you used to say the wrong things before now, even jokingly, it is time to take a step back and re-evaluate your words.

Always let your speech be seasoned with grace; this will attract the right people to you and cause you to be kind to yourself, as well. When words are used correctly, they become transformative tools.

7. Stick to Your Value System

Value systems are ideas we develop over time that help us maintain a certain standard of life. If you have value systems that have helped you shape your life in the most inspiring way possible, then now is the time to stick to them.

You shouldn't be moved by what everyone else is doing or what others adopt. Be determined to create your own rules and live by them. This is very important! People who are tossed around following other people's rules will never attain positive self-esteem.

Create a value system, stick to it and make it work; therein lies the pathway to high self-esteem.

Self-esteem is one of the most crucial yet underrated aspects of life. Everything a person will or will not achieve can be traced to how that person feels about himself. People with a very high perception of themselves tend to win all the time, not because they are somehow better, but because they believe in their abilities.

There is no telling how far one can go with very high self-esteem. It is akin to being the captain of a ship that is on course. Even if challenges come up later, the faith and hope you have built in yourself over time will help you put things in proper perspective and take the right steps.

Some of the principles discussed in this chapter will be presented in a very detailed form later, and we are starting with quiet acceptance. The next section contains lessons, tips, and valuable steps you can take toward cultivating high self-esteem via quiet acceptance. Do enjoy the read.

Chapter Two

Self–Acceptance; a Pathway to Cultivating High Self–Esteem

In discussing self-esteem, we must become aware of the role that self-acceptance plays. The previous section introduced you to some of the most basic concepts about the principles of self-worth - and quiet acceptance was listed.

Most cases of low self-esteem that manifest in people are as a result of a rejection of self, due to a feeling of being incomplete. If I build a house, I won't invite my friends over to the edifice until I feel it is 100% complete The same thing applies to us.

We often do not feel like we are enough. As such, we try to hide our most exact feelings because, just like the incomplete house, we feel as though we are not worthy of admiration or capable of doing anything right. We resort to self-rejection, and this affects our self-esteem.

Now that you have decided to build your self-esteem,

you must be willing also to accept all of you. Now, I'm not talking about only the best sides; I'm talking about all of you! No individual is born perfect, with every good trait. Some traits are acquired, others are impacted into you, and some others are inherited.

However, regardless of the traits you embody, you must appreciate who you are before you can start the process of developing your self-esteem. You are a unique personality; there is no one like you in your world. As such, you owe it to yourself to have very high self-esteem; one that allows you embrace every aspect of your life and live beyond your flaws.

Self-acceptance and self-esteem are not the same, but one leads to the other. If you love yourself well enough, there is an increasing chance that you will be able to build high self-esteem.

Self-acceptance is unconditional.

If you want to improve your self-esteem, you will need to explore the parts of yourself you are unable to accept. So, first you must stop passing judgement on yourself. Stop being so hard on yourself when you don't meet the expectations and targets you've set.

Self-acceptance can be traced back to the experiences

a person has as a child. As a young child, you probably didn't know anything about self-worth or self-esteem, so this is where your parents or guardians played a crucial role.

If your parents did a good job of making you feel unique, independent, and complete, you wouldn't have any challenge with self-love as an adult. The foundation was already laid.

However, if you were brought up in an environment where it seemed like nothing you did was right - an environment of constant abuse and lack of motivation, you would most likely develop a critical mindset about yourself.

The most refreshing idea thus far is the fact that you can cultivate self-acceptance. It is possible to learn how to embrace who you are and live in the moment while building up your self-esteem.

So, can we get right to the steps you'll take toward making this right? We will start now.

How to Become More Self-Accepting

1. **Cultivate Self-Compassion**

A person who wants to be self-accepting must be compassionate toward himself. Often, we show compassion to others, but we don't show the same to ourselves.

So, we make a mistake and boom! We criticise and even abuse ourselves emotionally. Be compassionate and kind to yourself by tolerating your flaws and excesses.

2. Be Inspired by Your Past and Not by Other People

You can build positive self-esteem when you are inspired by your own history. The only person you are in competition with is yourself. Your only goal is to outdo your past self. Ensure that at every turn, you are focused on yourself and not on others.

In order to be self-accepting, you must celebrate your past achievements and then look forward to achieving more in the future. If you are fixated on others, you will be putting yourself under intense pressure to become like them. This is not a good move toward cultivating self-esteem.

3. Forgive Yourself

People who struggle with self-acceptance often have issues forgiving themselves for the wrongs of the past. If you don't forgive yourself, you will always be held down by these thoughts.

Be willing to forgive what you've done to yourself as

well as to others. Forgiveness is a powerful tool that can help you become more self-accepting. Do not deflate your self-esteem by holding a grudge against yourself.

4. Make Changes (When Necessary)

There may be some areas of your life you want to change, especially concerning how you work or react to circumstances, or in your relationships with others. Be bold enough to make changes when such changes are needed.

If you leave things the way they are (especially when they are not right), you will be fuelling the dissatisfaction you have with your life and getting upset over something you have the power to change.

5. Be Happy with Yourself

Happiness is free; please take advantage of it! You must be extremely happy and satisfied with yourself to experience self-acceptance. Happiness is empowering, especially in your journey toward building self-esteem.

Share your happiness with others, as well. Create a world full of cheer -and don't stop until your whole world lights up with joy and the quiet acceptance of yourself.

If you aren't mindful of how well you accept yourself,

you just might become so critical of your actions that it leads to self-resentment. This book is a practical one - and that explains why there are many steps for each tip.

The best gift you can give yourself is bringing these words to life through constant practice. As you read, make up your mind to act on what you discover. You will become what you repeatedly do; so make a commitment to your journey toward better self-esteem today by becoming more accepting of yourself.

Living purposefully is the next stop on our journey; discover the connection between purposeful living and self-esteem in the next chapter.

Chapter Three

How to Live Purposefully

Living purposefully refers to the idea that a person is living for a goal or purpose that acts as a driving force every day. A life of purpose is a life lived from the inside out where dreams and aspirations become a reality.

Whenever I speak about purposeful living, I liken it to a person embarking on a road trip. A driver needs to have a destination in mind while navigating through the routes with a reliable map.

Now, if the driver does not have an idea where he is headed, the trip will be a futile attempt and accomplish nothing. A purposeful life is one with a sense of direction; you have a goal in front of you, and wake up every day taking strategic steps towards accomplishing that goal.

So at this point, I know you are wondering what this has to do with building self-esteem. Well, the answer to your inquiry is the aim of this chapter. You will discover the connection between self-esteem and living purposefully while adopting approaches that help you discover your purpose, thus giving your self-esteem a significant enhancement.

As opposed to popular opinion, the purpose of life isn't just to be happy. Of course, happiness is essential, but the most important thing about living is making a difference in your own life and that of others by fulfilling your purpose. This also means that you must discover your purpose before filling it.

When you discover what you should be doing with your life, you will have a broader sense of appreciation for yourself, thus enhancing your self-esteem. A person who is oblivious of his purpose in life will live a very defeated life; he will be at the mercy of chance, and this deflates self-esteem.

Think about it this way; someone who has discovered their reason for living wakes up filled with optimism knowing that he can do so much more with his life. So, he goes about his day conscious of his abilities and making changes while being excited about life.

On the other hand, a person without a sense of purpose wakes up feeling uninspired and unsure about his abilities. He doesn't know if he can do all that is required of him. This makes him feel less confident - and we all know that confidence is a significant ingredient in building high self-esteem.

The importance of living purposefully cannot be overemphasised.

You will discover steps you can take toward living purposefully such that your self-esteem is on a stable level. But first, you must provide answers to questions that will help you discover your purpose, as well as what it means for a person to live with a sense of direction. After this process, we will discuss tips on how to live purposefully and build high self-esteem.

Are you ready to take on this step our journey? I hear your loud yes!! Let's get started with some questions.

For you to live a purposeful life, you must ask yourself specific questions. The answers to these questions will serve as the compass you require to determine your purpose. Find these queries below:

1. What do I want to achieve?

2. How do I achieve it?

3. Are there steps I must take toward achieving it?

4. Does my environment have a role to play?

5. Is there novel information I need to adopt?

6. Should I adjust my strategies?

7. Who will help me fulfil this goal?

8. How long will it take?

9. What do I have to give up achieving it?

10. How can I sustain this purpose?

For a more meaningful experience working with these questions, you will need to get a journal where you can document your answers. After reading through this chapter, go back to the issues and answer honestly. Your answers will point you in the direction of how you should live your life.

What Does it Mean to Live with Purpose?

Lots of indicators show what living purposefully entails. Below, we will take on a few. Remember that all of these approaches are building up to helping you improve your self-esteem. So, for a person to live purposefully, he must take note of the following:

1. Oversee formulating goals consciously.

2. Identify and implement actions that are necessary for the achievement of set goals.

3. Monitor behavioural traits to determine if they

align with your goals.

4. Pay close attention to the results of your actions; it will help you determine whether you are making progress or not.

With purpose, you must continuously ask yourself: how do I move from here to get there? You also need to determine sub-purposes that will help you accomplish your goal.

Now to the big one! How can all these lessons you've learned become instrumental in helping you overcome low self-esteem and become the fearless Alpha-male you want to be? Read on; it gets better from this point.

How to Boost Self-Esteem by Living a Purposeful Life

1. Go for Your Goals Ferociously

You can defeat low self-esteem through purposeful living and going after your purposes fiercely. People with low self-esteem are mostly afraid of attacking their goals, and as such, they never accomplish anything.

You can improve your self-esteem by making sure your goals are a top priority through purposeful living. As you take deliberate steps toward achieving your purpose in life, you will be building an unshakeable self-esteem.

Let your goals inspire you to greatness as you live out your dreams every day.

2. Learn from Failures and Move On

As you become attuned with your goals, rest assured that you will make mistakes (this is how life works). Now, this is the problem with errors; some people become so upset by their failures that they don't want to try anymore.

When you allow failures to get the better part of your mind, you will experience low self-esteem. First, you need to tell yourself that it is okay to make mistakes, and even to fail - then make up your mind to move on from these mistakes.

Once you develop a positive mind-set toward failure, it will never have a hold over how you feel about yourself. Be open about failures; make them a part of your experience and learn.

3. Be Focused on the Future

Purposeful living entails being focused on the future. It is all about what you can do today to guarantee tomorrow's success. So, you must become consumed with the idea of having a better future.

Your self-esteem will get to a stable level when you become conscious of the fact that you can effect changes in your future now. It's like having superpowers - and superheroes have great self-esteem, right?

Always keep the future in focus; it will help you become an optimistic person who isn't afraid. The absence of fear means the presence of very good self-esteem.

4. Optimism is a Tool

Speaking of optimism, did you know that it is a tool? Oh yes, it is! Confidence is a tool that can be used to boost self-esteem while pursuing a life of purpose.

Individuals with low self-esteem will always be pessimistic, because they lack confidence. The solution is simple; get rid of the defeatist attitude, replace it with a cheerful disposition, and watch your self-esteem rise like an edifice.

Positivity will take you further; it will always make it possible for you to look beyond present obstacles and have a solution-driven mindset.

5. Always Aim High

If you are keen on living a purposeful life, that translates into great self-esteem. You must be willing to aim higher. Don't settle for less when you can have so much more.

6. Be in Control of Your Decisions

Being in control of your choices is a significant indicator that you have developed great self-confidence. Remember that this is your life and you must be willing to take charge.

A lack of controlled decision-making skills can lead to an absence of belief in one's ability to win in life. And this is a significant deal-breaker when considering self-esteem.

Trust in your ability to make the right decisions at all times, and remember what we talked about when we mentioned embracing mistakes. Even when you fail, never lose sight of the impact your choices have on your self-esteem.

7. Celebrate Your Wins

Above all, always celebrate your successes. Regardless of how little they may be, be happy with your milestones and be conscious of how far you have come, while always hoping for the best.

If you make a habit of celebrating your wins, you will observe a significant boost in your self-esteem. Celebrating your successes means you appreciate all the effort you've put in; this is a major self-esteem booster.

Be the person who embraces all his journeys; the highs and lows are a significant part of your experience, so be grateful for the former while staying optimistic for more of the latter.

We have succeeded in establishing a connection between self-esteem and living with purpose. There is so much for you to achieve when you know exactly what you are meant to do with your life. As you set yourself on fire with your goals, you will also be giving your self-esteem the boost it requires.

All the strategies you have gleaned in this chapter will only become effective when you start implementing them immediately. As you do, be mindful of the lessons you learn and use your experience to help someone else grow. We will be considering happiness in a moment; flip over to the next chapter to get all the scoop.

Chapter Four

Getting Rid of Happiness Anxieties

Happiness is crucial to living a great life. This is the reason a lot of self-help books always insist on the principle of being happy. If everyone could be happy forever, the world will be a better place. Some issues may come up that affect the quality of a person's happiness.

When a person isn't pleased, they will have to deal with low self-esteem. So in this chapter, we will deal with a significant concept that affects a person's happiness. We are talking about happiness anxieties.

Happiness anxieties can also be referred to as the fear of being happy, and it is a significant cause of low self-esteem. When a person is happy and fulfilled with life, they will always be optimistic, thus building up a great feeling of self-acceptance.

However, some people who have had hurtful experiences in the past try to justify why they shouldn't be happy. As such, they gradually build resistance toward being happy. This gives room for anxiety, panic attacks, and fear, all of which are factors that affect a person's self-esteem.

Happiness anxieties take time to build. It may start as a thought and then gradually increase to a feeling of discontent that triggers overall sadness. All of these negative emotions culminate into a person becoming sceptical of happiness.

The most vital point you should note here is this; happiness anxieties will affect your self-esteem in the most negative ways. What we should consider now is how to get rid of this feeling for good.

This chapter is a straightforward and practical one; you will discover steps you can take toward getting rid of your happiness anxiety. Please note that if you have been dealing with this anxiety for a while, it may take you a long time to get out of it. But if you are committed to the tips, they will work for you. Let's get started!

Note that for every step you will encounter below, there is an exercise you must carry out. Think of the activity as an accountability test that helps ensure you do what is required of you through the steps.

How to Get Rid of Happiness Anxieties

1. Think Happy Thoughts

First, you need to ensure that you are always thinking happy thoughts. Come on, how else will you fight off happiness anxieties if not with happy thoughts? You have got to be deliberate about this!

You cannot afford the luxury of one bad thought, so take it seriously. With happy thoughts, you can be sure of taking satisfactory actions that boost how you feel about yourself.

So, every day, there is a battle in your mind of the thoughts that will prevail; happy or sad feelings.

Exercise:

Every day, censor your thought process by ensuring that it is in line with what makes you happy. Whenever you feel like you are dwelling on an uninspiring thought, get it out of your mind and replace the idea with a happy one. Do this consistently, and you will be able to gain mastery over your thoughts.

2. Share Your Joy with Others

Life is worth living when you can share simple pleasures with others. As you think happy thoughts, share the feelings of joy with others around you. Those with very high self-esteem always have a touch, smile, or word of kindness for someone else.

You will be able to build very high self-esteem by being involved in the lives of others. And more importantly, this is one way of kicking out happiness anxiety.

Exercise:

What can you share with someone close to you? Think about how you can put a smile on that person's face - and go right ahead and do it. Remember that building self-esteem isn't just about what you do, but what you do for others.

3. Take the Pressure off Yourself

As you share your joy, remember to take the weight of pleasing others off yourself. In a bid to make everyone else happy, we put a great deal of pressure on ourselves. This affects our level of self-esteem.

At all times, remember to be yourself. It is okay to try your best for others - but not at the expense of mounting pressure on yourself unnecessarily.

Happiness anxieties will start to kick in when you put yourself under undue pressure. The exercise below will help you avoid this pitfall.

Exercise:

Whenever you start to feel pressured, take a deep breath, sit in a tranquil place, close your eyes, and take your mind off the pressure. After a few minutes, analyse the reason you feel pressured and deal with it by either getting rid of it or doing happily what can be done.

4. Choose to Say No

We just analysed the reason you shouldn't put yourself under pressure, but did you know that the urge to say yes to everyone is a form of coercion?

You are not obligated to listen to and endorse what everyone says, or else you will lose yourself in a bid to please them. One of the traits evident in people with low self-esteem is their inability to speak out, especially when they aren't comfortable with something.

Exercise:

The next time someone asks you for something or requests that you do something for them, search your inner self to decide if it is something you really want to do. Now, if you are excited about doing it, go right ahead. On the contrary, if you aren't so enthusiastic about it, make that clear to the person making the request. Saying NO is up to you!

5. See the Good in Yourself

There are good things you embody. Oh, I hope you will see all of you through your own eyes. When people see only their wrongs, they shrink in confidence.

We will speak more on embracing your flaws in the next step, but before we get there, I want you to become aware that you are blessed with a lot of great attributes. These great qualities you have will make you feel good about yourself.

Exercise:

Take some time to reflect on your life, identify those good things about yourself, and ensure that you amplify them by acting on them often.

6. Embrace Your Imperfections

Everyone is created with flaws, and if you are unable to embrace your faults, you will always seek perfection and be dissatisfied with your inability to attain it.

Be so in love with yourself that there is no room for self-condemnation. It is okay to look up to people you admire, but don't beat yourself up trying to be perfect.

Exercise:

What are those areas you feel are your imperfections?

Enjoy them today; they are a part of your life, so embrace them. The people you think have great self-esteem also have shortcomings, but they have been able to accept such flaws. Hence the reason they are so confident.

7. Be Conscious of Your Moods

Most times, feelings of anxiety manifest through our spirits. If you are always prone to severe mood swings, you will most likely experience happiness anxieties.

By paying attention to your moods, you can tell when you are sad, happy, or angry. Once you can tell how you are feeling, you will know how to adjust your mood to suit your goal of being happy.

Exercise:

How are you feeling now? Happy? Disappointed? Sad? Fulfilled? If you are in a happy mood, then keep up with the activities and thoughts that make you feel happy. If you are experiencing negative feelings, discover why you have such feelings and deal with them now.

8. Engage in Happy Activities

How important this is!

Happiness anxieties cannot thrive in an environment with peaceful activities. However, happy actions do not just happen. You've got to actively participate in them every day.

Happy activities vary from person to person. For some people, exercise makes them feel uplifted, while for some others, hanging out with friends work just fine. For you, it might be reading a book. But whatever it is, ensure that you do it often.

Exercise;

Think of an activity that makes you happy - and get on with it right now. Set a schedule to do it regularly within a specified period and you will be glad you did.

9. Be Kind to Yourself

We are raised to be helpful to others, to treat them well, and to be models of goodness to all those around us. But the real question is, are we kind to ourselves? Do we love who we are and who we have become?

It is so important to exercise kindness toward yourself, or else you will look for it in others. And when they fail to give it to you, you tend to suffer low self-esteem. Those things you do for others that exhibit kindness - do them to yourself as well.

Check on your emotions, buy gifts for yourself, and be patient with who you are becoming.

Exercise:

Use the remainder of the day to perform acts of kindness to yourself. Do something you have never done for yourself and watch your self-esteem get a significant boost.

10. Make Happy Decisions

The kind of decisions you make determine if you will be able to get rid of happiness anxiety. You must always be deliberate about making choices that cause you to be happy.

Of course, there will be times you will be required to make some decisions you are not entirely happy about. But, if MOST of your personal choices are happy ones, it will go a long way toward helping you retain happiness, thus building healthy self-esteem.

Exercise:

What decisions are you making at this very moment? Think of one and go back and review your desire to make this decision. Be sure that it is one you will be happy with long term. After reviewing your willingness to make the choice, only go through with what makes you happy. Get on this task now!

11. Be Comfortable with Your Life

Being satisfied with your life doesn't mean you shouldn't aspire to be and do more. It just means that you appreciate where you are right now and look forward to getting more out of life.

However, the key concept here is being happy with where you are in life. A lot of times, people develop poor self-esteem because they wish to become more like someone else. They are not satisfied with their lives, so they seek validation from others.

The problem with seeking validation is this; you will end up being uncomfortable with your own life and then attempt live out other people's dreams, thus leading to a miserable experience.

For you to guard how you feel about yourself, you must be comfortable with whatever level you are at right now. Your ability to be comfortable shows strength of character and that is what having high self-esteem is all about.

Exercise:

Get your journal and make a list of all the things you are very comfortable and happy with in your life. Ensure that you look back as far as five years. After writing, give yourself a thumbs-up and smile at your accomplishments, knowing that it will get better going forward.

Happiness anxiety is one of the major causes of low self-esteem. It starts with a thought and then gradually becomes a part of the person's mental process. Ultimately, the individual begins to feel downcast, and this erodes them of high self-esteem.

With the tips you have been given above, you can fight off the feeling and deal with the issue of being anxious over being happy. We are now done with the chapter on happiness, and our next stop is putting you in focus. Self-awareness is crucial, but how important is it? Get some answers to this and more in the next chapter.

Chapter Five

Being Conscious of Self

Justin has always known that he isn't a party person. He loves to be indoors and enjoys spending time by himself. However, he's got friends who are the "life of a party"; these friends must hang out every Friday -and every other day.

So Justin makes it to events with his friends every weekend. And when he gets home, he feels like he has wasted time doing nothing because he isn't a party person. The case with Justin is simple; he isn't conscious of who he is at all.

If Justin continues to violate who he is to please his friends, he will lose track of himself. This can lead to a very severe case of low self-esteem. By continually leaning on others and believing in what they uphold without having his own opinion or taking a stance, Justin will end up with very low self-esteem and a lack of self-confidence.

Self-esteem is about having a view of yourself that

allows you to feel great about who you are. It is a feeling that brings about confidence and a feeling of wholeness. But if a person isn't conscious of self, or isn't aware of who they are, there will be a problem.

Being self-conscious also means you have a sharp realization of your personality, strengths, weaknesses, beliefs, thoughts, motives, and emotions. When you are self-aware, you will be able to understand other people and discover how they perceive you, as well.

For you to be a man with very high self-esteem, you must first become aware of who you are. Now, this chapter is significant, so I will need you to pay very close attention.

When we speak of being self-aware, we refer to ideas around how well you know yourself. Make no mistakes about this; no one can attain high self-esteem without first knowing who they are. So here goes; WHO ARE YOU?

Take a few minutes to provide answers to that question.

Do you know who you are now? Do you know what you love? What do you appreciate about life? What can you not tolerate? What about the kind of people you relate easily with? How well do you know your emotions? How about your preferences? There are a whole lot of things you must consider when thinking about who you are.

If you do not get to know who you are, you will be a confused person who isn't able to hold his own anywhere. The key to building and maintaining high self-esteem is to discover who you are first - then ensure that the steps, actions, and activities you indulge in help bring out the best in who you are, thus aiding increased confidence.

In this chapter, you will come across two significant aspects. They include the benefits of being self-conscious and how a person can become self-aware. Beginning with the benefits, below you will find some of the reasons why it is essential for you to become self-aware.

The Benefits of Being Self-Conscious

1. It Helps You Become a Better Leader

Great leaders are self-conscious. They know that they must lead others, so they need to have a very firm grasp on their own strengths and weaknesses. As they discover themselves, they get to know more about those they lead.

2. Increases Self-Esteem

We are talking about how to build better self-esteem, so

we are on course as we discover more about ourselves. When you are aware of who you are, your self-esteem will increase.

At this point, you are not trying to be like someone else; nor are you modelling your life after someone else's dream. So, if you are ready to feel better about yourself, then you must learn to discover who you are by being self-aware.

Get to know you; the real you!

3. You Tend to Build Better Relationships

With knowledge of who you are, you will also develop better relationships because you will spend time with people of like minds. Justin would have made better choices with his friends if he had stayed true to who he was.

It is so important that you spend time with people who are like you or have the same belief systems as you. Life becomes more comfortable when you know what you want and the people around you are on the same page as you.

The quality of your relationships will be determined by the kind of people you spend time with. Don't accept or encourage any relationship that makes you feel pressured enough to do things you don't want to do. Relationships should change you for the better.

4. You Make Better Decisions

When you are self-aware, you make better decisions. Some people make poor decisions based on who others are rather than on who they are. This affects the results they get in life.

Instead of being led to make wrong decisions by other people, invest in getting to know yourself. You will be grateful for the time you spent learning about yourself as it will lead to better, healthier, and wiser choices.

5. You Minimize Mistakes

Although mistakes are inevitable, if you get to know who you are, this makes it possible for you to reduce errors. Some mistakes can be avoided if you pay attention to who you are long enough.

The pathway to living a life with fewer mistakes is being in touch with the real you, and not forgetting that this also serves as a significant boost for your self-esteem.

Now that you know the importance of being self-aware, we can get right to the focus of this chapter; how to become self-aware.

Aside from asking yourself questions that will help you discover who you are, you can engage in some fascinating steps that will give insight into how you can become more self-aware. Now remember that it isn't enough for you to become aware of who you are, you must also live out your truth.

Justin knew who he was but didn't act on that knowledge. Instead, he was carried away by the desires and wants of the people around him. So below, you will read through some of the most effective steps you can take toward becoming self-aware.

How to Become Self-Aware to Build Healthy Self-Esteem

1. **Practise Self-Reflection Every Day**

When you practise self-reflection every day, you will be able to better stay connected with who you are. You can practise self-reflection by taking time out of your schedule to discover who you are and what you want in life.

A good way of reflecting and engaging in exercise is through yoga. If you are not a fan of yoga, then you might want to find a quiet corner in your home where you can think, reflect, and discover.

Sometimes, people read about self-reflection, do it for

a week or two, and then put a stop to it; but it won't work like this. You've got to do it consistently to get the desired results.

More so, reflections can be done at the end of each day. Think about what happened to you and how the events of the day give an accurate picture of who you are.

2. Keep a Journal

Another way of being self-aware is keeping a journal. Now, this isn't a journal for secrets. I am talking about a memoir that chronicles your activities such that you can determine who you are from the entries.

If you are going to keep a journal, then it must be updated often. Write down important events and activities that happen and how you respond to them. These little efforts, if done repeatedly, will help you discover your true nature.

3. Work with Friends

Your friends see what you don't, sometimes. As such, it will be a great idea for them to provide feedback. Sometimes, we must look at ourselves through the eyes of someone else to know what we value and what we don't.

If you've got a great support system, you might want to have an assessment meeting with your friends. At such meetings, they will share their experiences and thoughts about you (the positives and negatives). You would do the same for them, so it's a balanced narrative.

At the end of such meetings, you will be amazed at all you will discover about yourself just by getting feedback from those nearest and dearest to you

4. Practise Meditation

We talked about reflecting earlier on, and that is entirely different from meditating. When you meditate, you keep your mind fixated on one thing, concept, or idea.

In this case, you will be meditating about your life. As you meditate, you will become aware of your inner powers and connect with yourself on a whole new level. That connection will help you maintain a great relationship with yourself that leads to very high self-esteem.

5. Be Objective with Yourself

Lastly, you've got to be objective with your self-assessment. Subjectivity will make you become biased towards yourself, and this won't help you on your journey to better self-esteem.

When you are objective, you will become real enough to point out your faults and be determined to work on them. Individuals who are objective tend to exhibit high self-esteem because they have conquered all fears.

If you are self-aware, you will be a man with very solid self-esteem. You will be able to embrace your strengths and weaknesses while staying true to who you are. In being conscious of who you are, you will require a very vital tool - the mind. Head over to the next section as you discover how the mind can be used in ensuring great self-esteem.

Chapter Six

Using the Mind as a Force Field

There is a connection between the mind and self-esteem.

You will ultimately become everything you think you are. So that means the mind is a forcefield that can be used to achieve desired results.

The mind is not a physical organ of the body, but a part of your make-up as a human being, and it contains information on all you think, dream and aspire to be. In your mind, you can become anything; whatever you feed it will show forth in your life.

This chapter takes us a step further in our journey by checking in with your psychological framework through the power of your mind. We will not make a lot of progress on this journey to better self-esteem if we don't consider the role the mind plays.

So, as you read through, get ready to discover some of the best ideas on how you can transform your life, kick depression out, and be the best version of all you can be, just by using your mind correctly.

A force field can serve as an invisible barrier that is used as a protective shield. Your mind can be a protective shield that keeps you safe from negative ideas that may affect your self-esteem.

There is so much to discuss in this chapter, and we will go through it because once you get it right in your mind, you get it right in every other aspect of your journey toward better self-esteem.

You should know that everything you experience in your life is as a result of what you have birthed in your mind. Have you ever thought about a person and then BOOM, you see that person within seconds of that thought? Well, that gives you an idea of how powerful the mind is. But more importantly, it teaches you the impact the mind has over everything you do.

Everyone is born with a mind, but not everybody can utilise it successfully. The mind can be trained and developed to function as a person wants it to; it is all about the kind of material you feed it.

So concerning self-worth, if you always tell yourself that you aren't good enough, you aren't worthy, and every other negative comment that doesn't add value to your experience, you will gradually begin to lose faith in yourself and develop a poor perception of who you are.

When we say the mind can be trained, what can we use as a tool to affect training?

Tools for Training the Mind

1. Words

Using words, you can feed your mind with negative or positive ideas that will determine the level of your self-esteem. You must have heard or been told about how you shouldn't use the wrong words on other people right?

Well, you really shouldn't use hurtful words on yourself, either. In a bid to be kind, ensure that you are always speaking kindly to yourself.

If your words do not teach or inspire you, they will settle in your mind like weeds in fertile soil. You may forget those cruel things you said, but the mind has absorbed them. Then, one day when you need motivation from within, instead of hearing the right words from your mind, those weeds speak up. And you already know that weeds are always up to no good.

Your self-esteem will develop in a positive light or diminish based entirely on your choice of words. You ought to listen attentively to yourself. What are you saying when no one else is around you? What do you mutter to yourself?

If you censor your words, you will also be able to protect your mind; and a guarded mind is a platform for increased self-esteem. Aside from the words you say to yourself, you should also be mindful of what others tell you. If you are always around people who bring you down with words, you may want to reconsider your circle.

A young man shared a story once of how he had to resign from his job because his boss was always verbally abusive toward him. So this boss knew that the young man was talented and good at his job but wouldn't want to give commendations.

At every turn, he found a way of bringing the young man down with hurtful and sarcastic comments. Gradually, this young man's self-esteem started to wane. The employee could no longer carry out tasks confidently; he had a lot of weeds in his mind as a result of all the negative words he heard.

When he resigned, he took time off to detoxify himself and replace those words that had destroyed his self-esteem with powerful affirmations that reminded him of who he was.

The mind is like a garden; your thoughts are the plants and words are like the water used to nurture the plant. However, if the words are not favourable, they become weeds that choke the garden and lead to deflated self-esteem.

Today, decide to only listen to the kind words because of the sanity of your mind. Say the right things to yourself, as well. Now, aside from words, there is another tool that is used for training the mind. You will find it below.

2. **Images**

The mind uses pictures to bring ideas to your consciousness. If you have been to Paris before and you want to tell someone about your experience, you will probably first think about the Eiffel Tower. That image will spur you on to narrate your experiences.

You see that the image of the tower remains stuck in your mind because it is indeed a sight to behold. The pictures in your mind also go a long way in determining how you feel about yourself.

There is a viral photo of a cat looking at a mirror, and the reflection it sees is that of a lion. This photo aptly captures the power of images to the mind. That cat will always move and act like a lion. It is fearless and utterly confident because the image it sees in the mirror inspires faith.

It isn't about what the reality is when we are dealing with the mind. Instead, it is all about what you see and perceive to be real. So, if you see yourself as a failure who isn't going to achieve much, then rest easy knowing that whatever is left of your self-esteem will be destroyed.

Ensure that at every chance you get, you show your mind uplifting images of yourself. You've got to be deliberate about this; don't allow the wrong picture to settle in the force field of your mind.

We have already established the fact that self-esteem is a crucial ingredient for success. As such, if you are going to succeed, you must be willing to protect your mind at all costs.

Now, images can also come from the media; sometimes the media likes to portray men as being weak especially in a world where lots of women are beginning to shatter glass ceilings. As you read through what the media offers, make sure you filter the images that settle in your mind.

When your mind is free from negative words and images, you will be able to truly live out your potential as an Alpha male who is fearless and willing to take on the world.

In dealing with the mind, we should also consider the role of mental health, because this plays a considerable role in shaping how you feel about yourself.

Words and images are tools you can use in shaping the narrative within your mind; once you've got great words and images, you must start thinking about how you can improve your self-esteem using the right frame of mind.

How to Use the Mind to Improve Your Self-Esteem

1. **Learn to be Assertive**

Being assertive means you don't have ideas and words you want to share clogged up in your mind. It means you can speak and say precisely what you want to say at any time.

As an assertive person, your mind will be free of insecurity, and you will become bold enough to speak and share your thoughts confidently. As you speak with boldness, your self-esteem receives a significant boost, and that is what you need to become fearless and daring.

2. 2. Focus on the Positives

You can use your mind as a tool for focus. Be mindful of the positive things that happen around you and feed your mind with such details.

Whatever you focus on consistently will have a significant impact on how your mind embraces the idea of having improved self-esteem. Make it a routine to delete all traces of negative energy or thoughts at the end of each day.

Welcome every new day with optimism and a renewed desire to get the best out of your mind. Improving on your self-esteem is a process; work at it every single day and enjoy the results afterwards.

3. Recreate Your World

It is possible to recreate your world if you are not satisfied with what you experience currently. For some people, they've got a positive mindset, but their personal lives do not correspond with what they envision in their minds.

If you are not happy with what you've got now, have a reorientation of the mind and recreate your world. Your mind can become a world of possibility and reality to you; use it to fire up your self-esteem, and you will be grateful you did.

4. 4. Fall in Love with Yourself

Love makes everything alright with the world, and love can give you the self-esteem boost you require. So, now you need to love yourself more than ever before. We will elaborate more on how you can fall in love with yourself in a later chapter, so look out for that.

As you love yourself, you will discover all those great things about you that you appreciate and that make you feel good about yourself. People who are in love with themselves do not bring themselves down with hurtful words.

Let your mind become a force field of love that is nurtured and groomed in such a way that there is no room for anything contrary. Love is the most powerful emotion that can transform a man's life. But more importantly, self-love is crucial to adopting high self-esteem.

5. 5. Create Mental Boundaries

Mental boundaries refer to the barricades you set up that prevent the wrong ideas, images, and thoughts to breed in your mind. Because your mind is all-powerful, you need to be sure that only the good stuff gets in.

Your mental boundaries can be counter-words and

actions that repel the effect of the wrong things on your mind. For every unhappy thought that tries to get to your mind, counter it with a happy thought; this is how you use mental boundaries to protect your mind and boost self-esteem.

If the mind is nurtured and protected, it can be used as an instrument for improved self-esteem. With the information you have received in this chapter, the onus lies on you now to ensure that your mind is not left to roam freely, accepting any image or word.

Once you create mental boundaries, recreate the world you desire, and fall in love with yourself, you will be able to use your mind to improve your self-esteem. Remember to focus on the positives while learning how to be assertive. The next section reaffirms the power you hold as an individual; it is one section you don't want to miss.

Chapter Seven

You are Enough!

One of the reasons some people suffer from very low self-esteem is because they don't think they are enough and they always seek validation from others.

The issue of seeking validation from others was mentioned briefly in a previous chapter, but here we will analyse it thoroughly. People do not enjoy the benefits of self-esteem because they are looking at someone else and thinking that what that person has is what they need to feel complete.

So the struggle for wholeness begins, and the further the journey goes, the more such individuals imitate others, the more they lose themselves in the process. What is left of them is a man who is afraid, tired, and depressed - because no one can be like someone else.

We are all born with unique traits and abilities. What you can do if you are not satisfied with what you have is to improve on yourself, so you become better instead of trying to be like somebody else. Hear me say this to you now; YOU ARE ENOUGH!!

There is no one else like you in the world! That should be enough reason for your self-esteem to be at a very high level. The temptation to be like someone else will only drive you into losing your originality.

When you start to exhibit the traits of someone else, you will develop a deep feeling of dissatisfaction because you realise that you are only an imitation and not an original. The world has embraced technology, and through avenues such as social media, we are exposed to many people who live false lives.

Here you are being authentic and real with your story, and then because you follow this person on Instagram, who seems to have a "perfect life," you suddenly feel like you don't have anything.

The quest to imitate someone with the perfect life begins, and as you try to do your best with the information dished out on social media, you lose the essential part of your life that makes you unique. I am not saying that you shouldn't be on social media, but be mindful of what you adopt because it may affect your self-esteem in the long term.

Always tell yourself that you are enough. You may not be where you want to be, but you are not where you used to be. An important criterion needed for a person who wants to have very high self-esteem is to be content with who he is.

There is so much power in being happy with who you are; it not only helps you gain improved self-esteem, it also enables you to experience satisfaction with your life in general.

No matter how much I tell you that you are enough, it will not make a lot of impact unless you believe it and say it to yourself as well. A deeper appreciation of who you are will be instrumental in helping you build and sustain a great self-image.

Being enough also means that you like yourself (this is a more straightforward way to put it). You have got to be comfortable in your skin, smile at the mirror more, and generally love who you are - because it is only when you accept yourself that you can start building great self-esteem.

So, what can you do to internalise this message of being enough? Oh, you can do a whole lot; and we are getting to it right now. Below, you will read through the top eight strategies you can practise and adopt that which will help you like yourself more, so you can say you are enough and mean it.

Top Eight Steps on How to Like Yourself and Develop High Self-Esteem

1. Talk to Yourself as a Friend

One of the steps toward loving yourself and reinforcing the message of being enough is by talking to yourself as you would a good friend. As a friend to yourself, emphasise those traits and attributes you embody that make you unique.

When your friend continually gives you compliments, it boosts your confidence and aids in building better self-esteem, too. So, don't wait for your friend to tell you who you are. Be a friend to yourself; be your own best friend.

As you show kindness through words to yourself, you will always be content with who you are while improving on the areas you should work on.

2. Lower Expectations

When your expectations are too high, you will never feel like you are enough. Overly high expectations will make you feel like you are inadequate; and this negatively affects self-esteem.

Sometimes, it pays to lower your expectations - especially with ideas that will make you do things you aren't comfortable with, to meet up with the standards of other people.

Vet every expectation you have by ensuring that it is in line with what you want for your life and not some dream inspired by the need to be like someone else.

When expectations are lowered, you also get to appreciate the value of experience. Instead of rushing off to accomplish things, you will take pride in learning and growing through the process.

3. Visualise Yourself Getting Better

The key to liking yourself even more is in utilising the power of visualisation. You have to first see yourself the way you want to be before you can become that image.

Always visualise yourself getting better, increasing your capacity, and living an inspiring life. Most people do not use their minds to create the pictures they desire, so there is usually a gap between what they want and what they experience.

As you visualise, you also reposition yourself to take

strategic steps to bring the visions to reality.

4. Discover Who You Are

The only way you will learn to like yourself is by discovering who you are. You cannot want or love what you don't know; and regardless of how old you are, it is possible that you haven't discovered yourself yet.

This step is so important! You need to spend time discovering everything about yourself, so when you say "I am enough" it is said with authority.

You can discover who you are by spending time with yourself, analysing your responses to situations, and getting to know the kind of things you like. Once you find out how awesome you are, you will fall in love with yourself.

5. No Regrets

Regrets have a way of diminishing your self-esteem, especially when you fester on them for too long. So, make up your mind not to have regrets over situations you cannot control.

There will be times when you make mistakes; what you should do is learn from them and move on. The more you dwell on regrets, the more your self-esteem is affected negatively.

Make up your mind today to live a life that is without regrets. Whatever you experience is not a failure; it is only a lesson that will inspire you to become a better person.

6. Gratitude is a Lifestyle

In life, there will be ups and downs. But one thing is for sure, if you make gratitude a lifestyle, you will be amazed at how far you'll come. Be grateful for the little things, because the little things put together make the big things work.

Express gratitude to those who make the process easier for you, and be grateful for the challenges as well. Recognition helps you build and sustain great self-esteem, because you become aware of your imperfections and still appreciate your journey.

7. Use Affirmations

Oh, I love this step - because it works all the time. With statements, you can bring all you dream about, imagine, or desire to life. I always advise people to have an affirmation book that contains words about what they want.

Every day, they say these words to themselves, and it forms the basis on which their self-esteem lies. Affirmations are not said so you'll believe them; they are said because you already have faith in your words.

If you have struggled with being punctual in the past, you can write affirmations that state how early you always are to events. Gradually, you will observe that you are indeed becoming a punctual person.

If you feel like you are dealing with low self-esteem, then now is the time to write out affirmations that express high self-esteem. Keep saying what you believe, and it will become a part of you eventually.

8. Bring Out the Good in You

As you discover and affirm who you are, take steps toward bringing out the very best in yourself. Men with very high self-esteem showcase the good within them in the most humbling ways.

If you are good at something and you find yourself in a place where such skills are needed, don't shy away from offering to help. Speak up and do your best to make a difference. As you do these little things for others, you will be building confidence in yourself

Once you tell yourself that you are enough, repeatedly, it will become a truth that you endorse and believe. Your self-esteem will also experience a significant boost as you bask in the thrill of being enough.

No one should have to aspire to be somebody else. Yes, you can admire people and want to emulate them; but don't desire to copy them entirely, because you are an original. As you maintain your stance on being enough, be prepared to fight and win the war within; this and more await you in the next section. Do enjoy the read.

Chapter Eight

Winning the War Within

If there is anything Ashton doesn't like about deciding, it is the process of choosing what to do at a given time. So, whenever he is faced with a tough choice to make, he tries to avoid it; and this is a sign of very low self-esteem.

The more Ashton avoids issues that require him making a choice, the more his self-esteem wanes. Ashton's inability to decide stems from the fact that he hasn't dealt with the war that rages on within him.

Until he wins that war, he will be plagued by indecisiveness, which happens to be a factor associated with low self-esteem. There are a lot of Ashton's in the world today. People who struggle with themselves daily are unable to get anything done.

The first concept you should grasp here is simple; there is a war that rages on inside you. If you don't manage it appropriately, you will make uninformed decisions and sometimes fail to make any decision at all.

What is this war really about?

Well, within you, there is a feeling of being torn between what you should do and what is expected of you. This war is usually a result of what you knew while growing up, your present environment, and what you know right now.

When you are faced with a problem, your first impulse is to think about what to do. You may not want to say the first idea that popped in your head, because you are trying to be careful. But, the more you shy away from making a decision, the more vulnerable you become, and the less you accept yourself.

There is always a constant battle from within that makes us appear confused, thus making it easy for people to take advantage of us. People will want to ride on the fact that you are always indecisive. Your ability to win the war will determine if you can protect yourself from them, as well as become a man who knows what he wants and goes for it.

In this chapter, you will be armed with steps to win the battle from within. You will be faced with other external factors, but if you can take care of what's within, then every other aspect can be handled.

How to Win the Battle Within

1. **Know What You Want**

Confusion and an inability to make great choices stems from the fact that people do not know what they want. When you see what you want and embrace the totality of your choices, you will be taking the first step toward winning the internal battle.

So, as you reflect and discover who you are, also get to know the things you want. When faced with the task of deciding, you will know exactly what to say and what to choose.

An Alpha Male isn't held down by indecision; your responsibility is to fight it off entirely by knowing what you want and going for it.

2. **Say It as It Is**

When you discover what you want, the next step will be for you to say it as it is when asked. The funny faces we make when we are asked a simple question are an indication that we are stalling because we are unable to express ourselves.

The war within causes you to ignore what you want to say because you are concerned with what people will think. Well, you really cannot become a great person with high self-esteem if you are always worried about what people think. Say what you want to say and damn the consequences.

3. Be Known for Being Confrontational

A lot of times, we are held back from building self-esteem because we try to avoid being confrontational. Instead, we murmur and talk behind others' backs - which is a bad trait.

People with very high self-esteem are known to look others in the eye and say what they want to say. When you are confrontational, you will always live freely with others.

Being confrontational makes it easy for you to be straightforward with others, thus building your self-esteem. Don't hold the grudge you've got for someone else. Walk up to them and solve issues; it is the hallmark of high self-esteem.

4. Don't Hold Yourself Back

At times when you need to express yourself, nothing should hold you back. Think about yourself at this point like a bird that is free to fly. Nothing should clip your wings, so hop on the side of self-esteem.

The more you let yourself go, the more likely you are

to improve your self-confidence. The key to being happy with yourself is to live freely; once you conquer this, every other thing falls into place.

As we round off this sub-section, remember to be free; it is a significant requirement for success on this self-esteem journey.

5. Make Smaller Decisions

Sometimes you dive right into making big decisions without first conquering the smaller ones. When you gain mastery over smaller decisions, you will be able to make the bigger ones with ease.

What to wear, what to eat, or what to do with your spare time are examples of small decisions. These are choices you make every day; so use them as opportunities to develop a stronger mindset towards decision-making.

6. Stick to What You Say

Often, we say something, and then we go back on it because we are not confident enough in ourselves. So, there are cases of people who say what they want to say, then when they are confronted before a larger audience, they deny their statement.

The solution to this challenge is quite simple; stick to what you say. If you want to avoid the devastating effect of being unsure about what you mean to people, own up to your statements.

Be known as a person who is always bold enough to make decisions and speak up regardless of what you are faced with. Your ability to stick to what you say is an indication of your high self-esteem.

7. Drown the Voice of Doubt

The voice of doubt will always be heard, but you should not give in to it. Whatever you decide, you will always feel unsure at some point. But you must drown that voice and not allow it to reign over your mind.

Self-esteem is about self-control and acceptance of one's own views. You cannot say you accept your views when your mind is filled with doubt. Get doubts off your mind by ensuring that you maintain a stern approach to everything you believe in.

Doubt makes you question everything and while having such questions is normal, nursing questions that make you lack faith in yourself is not ideal.

8. Be Firm with Others

People with low self-esteem tend to allow others to ride on them. You must be firm in the relationships you build with others. It is okay to accept suggestions from people, but when you make a final decision, be FIRM!

Do not be easily persuaded and tossed about doing the biddings of other people;, only people with low self-esteem live like that. When you show firmness with every decision you make, you will be able to build up great self-esteem.

9. Exude Confidence in Decision Making

While sharing your ideas with others via decision making, exude confidence. Always speak with clarity and look into others' eyes while you speak. You will be taken more or less seriously based on how confidently you express yourself.

The battle within is always based on what you should say, do, or accept -and confidence is one tool that will help you win. Faith isn't just about how you speak, but also about your body language.

If you speak with your shoulders slumped and eyes looking down, you will appear as someone who can be manipulated easily.

I know this book is replete with information on the role that confidence plays in building self-esteem, but this is because confidence and self-esteem are two peas in a pod; one cannot do without the other.

10. Trust Your Instincts

Your instincts will always be right. The thing about winning the battle within is the fact that you are not entirely helpless. You've got several tools at your disposal, and your instincts are one of such devices.

Whenever you are in doubt, rely on what your instincts tell you and use them to make your final decision. If you have trained your mind well to accept right over wrong, your abilities will never lead you in the wrong direction.

You have all you need to believe in yourself and trust the process.

The battle within is all about how you make decisions because your decision-making skills reflect how high or low your self-esteem is. People who are known for making great choices often show very high self-esteem, and you can too if you stick to the steps provided above.

Remember that the journey to improved self-esteem is a gradual one that entails a lot of work. You have read and implemented a lot of the steps, but still have a long way to go.

Upon winning the battle within, the next step in your journey is becoming responsible toward reality. There is so much for you to gain in the next section; head over there now for additional insight.

Chapter Nine

Being Responsible Toward Reality

In life, there are two facets to living; what we desire and what is real.

What we desire resides in our minds, it is a complete make-up of thoughts and ideas that we reach for daily in the quest to become better. For example, you may desire a Ferrari because it is a great car that shows elegance.

However, the reality of the situation is that you may not be able to afford a Ferrari. That means there is often a gap between desire and reality. What we want is not always want we can get and what we can get may not be what we desire.

This concept plays a significant role in the attainment of self-esteem, because for some people, their inability to get the things they desire makes them feel inadequate. This affects their self-esteem negatively.

In this chapter, we will consider the ways in which you can become responsible for reality. So clearly, the focus isn't just on our desires, because desires can be very misleading.

Before we get to the practical aspects of this chapter, I want you to understand how desires work. Desires spring upon us; they are like fantasies, wishes, and ideas we get that inspire a need within us.

You can be walking down the street and pass by an ice-cream shop; suddenly you want to get ice-cream. Now, before you saw the shop, there was no craving for ice-cream or anything cold. So what makes you want it so badly that you spend money getting it immediately? It's DESIRE!

When desire is left uncontrolled, it can lead to dire consequences and a constant battle with your reality. The goal for anyone who wants to improve self-esteem should be to welcome desires - but know when to indulge such feelings and when not to.

Back to the connection this has with self-esteem. If you are unable to buy the ice-cream at the time and also unable to purchase several other things you desire consecutively, it will have a significant impact on your self-esteem.

You start to feel like you are being deprived of things

others enjoy. The more you think that way, the worse you feel about yourself - and then you start to lose confidence.

The solution to all of these is simple; be responsible enough to know what YOUR REALITY is and stick to it. Remember that your reality may be different from that of your friend who may be able to afford all of his desires.

The concept of desire isn't restricted to just items you can buy, but the experiences and skills you want to enjoy. There are times you may have to take a break from certain activities, and in those times, you must never allow the feeling of not doing these things to affect your self-esteem.

Once you embrace your reality, life becomes less complicated. You no longer feel pressured to do things because other people are doing them. Instead, you are comfortable with where you are currently, knowing that your desires may not be fulfilled instantly but will be eventually.

Now, that's another thought process for you to explore. If you realise that you will get every good thing you deserve eventually, you will not be in a hurry to accomplish all you want immediately.

When you are responsible for your reality, you will be

taking the pressure off of yourself to impress others and alter what you can do. Now that you have an understanding of how desire and reality connect, the next step should be how you can become responsible for your reality. So here goes:

How to be Accountable for the Truth

1. **Be Content**

When you are content with what you have, it becomes easier for you to be responsible for your reality. Appreciate where you are as you reach for more, but be satisfied with the process.

Contentment makes it possible for you to stick to only what your reality can afford. As such, you tend to be happy with your decisions and still keep your self-esteem intact.

Always make decisions from a place of contentment. It is a pathway to ensuring a good life, especially if you are keen on building solid self-esteem.

2. **Take Charge of Your Desires**

Your desires shouldn't have rule over you at any time. Always take charge of how you feel and be in control of what you choose to do and what you choose not to do.

Instead of being carried away by your desires, build resistance within yourself by sticking to what is essential. One of the most vital signs of a person who has got great self-esteem is the ability to stay in charge regardless of what happens around them.

3. Build Resistance

For you to be responsible for your reality, it is essential that you build strength against some things early enough. You know, those things that affect you personally and cause you to stick to desires over reality; develop a healthy mindset against them.

Some people are described as being strong-willed. Such a description speaks of someone who is not easily moved by anything. So regardless of what you come across, you maintain the same disposition, and this is how you build very stable self-esteem.

4. Be Surrounded by Like-Minds

If a person who is shopaholic hangs around others like them, they will never change. So, if you spend time with people who cannot be responsible for their reality, you will also become a victim of your desires.

While you work on yourself and your self-esteem, do not forget or neglect the power of people. Anyone you are close to wields considerable influence over your life (positively or negatively).

Until you become mindful of the kind of people you spend time with, you will not be able to distinguish between desires and reality.

5. Plan, Plan, Plan

When you don't plan, you automatically set yourself up for problems. You can completely eradicate the issues that pop up with desires and reality just by planning carefully.

Plan for everything you want to do or purchase and after that, ensure that you stick to the program. So, if you already have a plan of what to do about the items you want to shop for, there will be minimal or no desires to reach for what isn't in your plan.

With planning, you can build and maintain a stable lifestyle that doesn't cause you to experience low self-esteem or dissatisfaction with yourself over your inability to get what you want.

6. Learn the Art of Compromise

Sometimes, all you need to do is compromise a little to get the desired results. Come on! Life is about compromise, especially when it is done for the greater good.

You may have to let go of something irrelevant (your desires) for something even better (your reality). When you start to compromise, you will begin to understand how things play out effortlessly with the right strategies.

With compromise, you will most certainly be giving up the worse option for the best and the more often you do this, the higher your chances of building stronger self-esteem.

7. Substitute Your Desires

At other times, all you must do is substitute your desires. For example, if you cannot get the Ferrari you want, what other vehicle can you use that will give you the same feeling of satisfaction the Ferrari offers?

It is all about being happy at the end of the day, and one of the fastest ways to become satisfied as you love yourself and improve on your self-esteem is by knowing when to substitute an item or experience that doesn't fit into your reality.

Substituted desire also means you get to satisfy your hunger for more, but in the most comfortable way. In the end, you will be happy for the substitution.

8. Set Goals

Goals are like plans. They are the ideas you have before setting the program in motion. So, with goals, it becomes possible for you to streamline what you want and stick to it.

As you set goals for yourself, you will be training your mind to get used to the process of planning, thus eliminating spontaneous impulses that encourage irresponsibility toward your reality.

You can build self-esteem that isn't affected by petty things just by being responsible and deliberate about accepting your reality. Go for what you want after you have calculated the risks and mapped out strategies on how you can keep your high self-esteem intact while making individual decisions.

Aside from being in touch with your reality, you have to also embrace the concept of learning consistently because that is a crucial ingredient for building great self-esteem. Learning never ends; get set to learn some more as you head over to the next section now.

Chapter Ten

A Commitment to Learning Always

Building self-esteem is a process. Sometimes it is a lifelong endeavour that doesn't have an end. If you are committed to it, you will always have something new to spice things up. Some people climb up the ladder, cultivate very good self-esteem, and yet they are unable to sustain it for the long haul.

We will address the issue of sustenance in another chapter, but before we get there, you should know that for you to attain heights with self-esteem and continue with it, they must be willing to take on the path of learning.

What are you doing right now? You are reading through material that is instrumental in helping you become a man who is fearless, daring, and ready to achieve big things. By reading this book, you have shown your desire to learn; but it doesn't end with one book.

Now that you know some of the principles of building self-esteem, you need to become even more committed to learning, because life is very dynamic. The people you meet, the places you go, and the experiences you have all affect your self-esteem at some point.

So, for you to continue the path you have set for yourself and the precedence you have set with this book, there is a need for continuous learning and growth.

The books you will read five years from now, and the podcasts and messages you will listen to in the future about self-esteem will contain a different word. Because there will be a lot of changes in your life then, you will also have to adopt new measures.

Anyone who has ever succeeded at anything will tell you that the educational and growth process never ends. You start it, and then you have a responsibility to uphold the process by going for more knowledge.

When something is important to you, you create time to work at it until you achieve your goals. So how important is this self-esteem issue to you? Are you willing to make it a major priority in your life? Are there steps required of you that you have made? Do you reach out for more?

The answers to the questions above will determine if you will continue with this chapter. Well, if you are ready to take on the process by learning continually, ensure that you take the tips you will find below seriously.

How to Improve Your Commitment to Learning

1. **Read Books**

The wisdom and knowledge of this world is found in books. If you aren't reading, you are dying. All religious sects in the world have their laws and rules contained in a "Holy book," because books are a symbol of true wisdom.

If you are going to learn more about self-esteem, you will need to read books about the subject matter — thumbs-up to you for reading one now, but don't allow this to be the last one. So off you go to the library and bookshops as you take your time searching for books about self-esteem.

Aside from physical copies of books, you should also get e-books that can be downloaded on your mobile phone, so you can read on the go. Subscribe to magazines that handle issues around self-esteem and you will be glad you did.

2. **Listen to Podcasts on the Go**

There are numerous podcasts on self-esteem. The most inspiring thing about podcasts is the fact that you can listen from anywhere in the world.

As you listen, you will feel a distinct connection to the speaker that makes it seem as if you are sitting right next to them as they admonish you on building self-esteem.

Podcasts are becoming very popular these days, especially in a world where technology is the most viable tool. What are you waiting for? Get your data-enabled phone, laptop, or mobile device and download podcasts you can listen to today as you make progress with your self-esteem.

3. Read Biographies of Great People

The most successful people in the world also have stories of how they overcame their self-esteem challenges. One very productive way of learning is by reading through their biographies to discover some of the steps they took in becoming more confident.

As you read through biographies, you will discover patterns among these great people and gain insight into how they shattered expectations just by believing in themselves.

If you have never read a biography before, today is a good day to read about someone who inspires you. Learning about other people is a sustainable means of maintaining all the lessons you have gleaned thus far.

4. Utilize Search Engines

Search engines such as Google are an excellent platform for learning. You can research anything and learn how to build confidence. Search engines offer a wide range of options when it comes to knowledge.

By just typing "How to improve my self-esteem," you will be exposed to a myriad of options, steps, tips, and lessons that will inspire you to take the right steps and do the right things to ensure maximum results.

A search engine is what is standing between you and what you don't know. Use it today and take your learning further.

5. Listen to Others Share Their Stories

There are people around you who have experienced their own self-esteem journeys. By listening to them, you will learn lessons and pick out one or two tips that will inspire your trip.

So, learn to pay attention to others, and you can get people to share their unique stories by also sharing yours. Whenever you get an opportunity to converse with someone, talk about self-love or confidence - something that will encourage them to also share their experiences.

As you listen to others share, you will be inspired to

take the right steps.

6. Join a Self-Esteem Group or Create One

If there are little groups on your street or in your office that comprise people coming around to share their experiences, join and contribute as you also listen to others.

However, if there are no self-esteem groups around you, create one! With all you have gained from this book, you can organize a reading club where you can share the content of this book with other men.

At such reading clubs, people should be given an opportunity to share their unique experiences; through this method, everyone learns, and everyone gains something from each other, as well.

7. Follow Self-Esteem Coaches on Social Media

Numerous coaches on social media can help you improve your self-esteem. If you are an avid social media user, all you need to do is search for such coaches and follow them.

Some of their tweets, posts, and videos are free. You can comment on their pages and get instant responses while interacting with other followers and users who want to improve their self-esteem as well.

Through social media, there is so much a person can learn if willing.

Don't waste the opportunity by being complacent.

8. Learn from Your Mistakes

A mistake is a sign that you are trying. The best thing you can do is learn from your mistakes, make the resolution to be better, and refuse to hold yourself back because of them.

The learning process entails you sometimes going overboard with plans or not even doing anything at all. Whatever the case will be, ensure that you are always learning from the things you fail at.

With a mindset to learn, you will view mistakes as opportunities to improve. Remember that improving one's self-esteem is a life-long process. It gets better gradually; it does not happen in one day. The more mistakes you make, the closer you get to your goal.

9. Subscribe to a Mailing List

If you subscribe to a mailing list sent by an expert on self-esteem issues, you will have an opportunity to learn from that person periodically. Mailing lists are also excellent because they offer a unique chance to get first-hand information from self-esteem professionals.

With every email you get, digest the content and add value to your experience by reading and learning. You can also share what you have learned with others; this will make the lessons stick with you for a longer period of time.

10. Get a Mentor

Everyone needs a mentor!

At this stage of your journey, you need a mentor who will hold your hand and guide you through this process. Your mentor should be someone who has also had the same self-esteem experience and overcome it graciously.

If you find such a person, reach out to them and you never know, you might get a great mentor who is willing to help you. As a mentee, you have a responsibility to listen to your mentor, ask questions, and follow through with everything you are taught.

Mentorship is a sure way to continue learning and to improve on all you have gained thus far.

Education is one aspect of life that never ends; you start learning from the day you were born and it doesn't stop until you die. So, make your self-esteem journey have the same lifelong process as you implement all you have discovered in this chapter.

Did you know that addictions have a firm hold on how you feel about yourself? The next section seeks to elucidate on how habits affect self-esteem; there are so many other ideas to be shared in that section, so head over there now and get started.

Chapter Eleven

Kicking Addictions Out

Addiction is the primary cause of low self-esteem. If you have ever been addicted to something before now, you should know that one of the reasons why you struggled with the addiction is because you weren't confident in yourself and your ability to overcome the challenge.

Addictions usually start as habits. At first, they may even seem like simple indulgences that don't affect you, but gradually they begin to get the best of you and take over your life.

There are two things we must consider when placing addiction and self-esteem side by side. First, some people become addicted to certain things because of low self-esteem. Second, some escape addiction and battle with low self-esteem.

There has been a recognized relationship between self-esteem and addiction for decades. Drug users were found to have low self-esteem, and this explains why they rely on the effects of drugs to stimulate a temporary sense of confidence.

People who are addicted to the Internet, eating, compulsive buying, and even pornography all suffer from low self-esteem. When they indulge in their addictions, their insecurities are masked, and they enjoy short-lived feelings of confidence. This shrinks their self-esteem even more in the long term.

So in the end, addictions are a terrible influence on your self-esteem. This chapter is an efficient one; you will read through steps and tips on how you can avoid both self-esteem pitfalls concerning addictions.

First, we will consider how to avoid getting addicted as a result of low self-esteem. Then, we will discuss how to build self-esteem after an addiction. By the time we get to the end of this chapter, you will be a brand-new man who is ready with a clean slate.

Now, if you are reading and you have never had any experiences with addiction, you might feel like you want to pass on this chapter, but I want you to hold it right there for a moment.

You may not be dealing with addiction right now, but you may know someone who is fighting to be free from it.

Remember that you are not only reading for yourself; you are reading and learning to make an impact in the lives of others as well.

So, if you have issues with addiction, read on. And if you don't have problems with addiction, read so you can lift someone else up. We will begin with the first phase of the journey to getting free of addiction so low self-esteem can be a topic of the past.

How to Avoid the Pitfall of Addiction from Low Self-Esteem

1. Focus on Yourself

When you discover that you are getting close to becoming addicted to something, try to focus on yourself even more. Some people will instead spend time with the material or event that leads them to full-blown addiction - and this is where the problem starts.

By paying attention to yourself, you will be able to deduce why you are feeling less confident - thus handling the issue from the moment it begins.

2. Find the Causes of the Problem

Now that you have total focus on yourself, you need also to discover the cause of the problem. Why are you feeling this way? Why is your self-esteem at an all-time low?

When you are determined to find answers, you will figure out the challenge.

The cause of the problem will most likely be something that makes you uncomfortable, so analyse your life and fish out those things that make you unhappy or uncomfortable; this is where the problem lies.

3. Talk to Someone

Don't wait until you start indulging in the addiction before you speak with someone who can help. A drowning man calls out for help, so reach out to someone who can help you at this phase before it's too late.

When you speak with someone, you will be able to share your burden, have a shoulder to lean on, and get advice as well.

4. Avoid Spending Time Alone

In times like this, you shouldn't waste time alone. Be surrounded by people, friends, and family who want the best for you. When you isolate yourself, the thoughts of addiction are reinforced, and this can pose a significant problem for you.

So, get out of the house, hang out with your dearest pals, and build meaningful relationships that will serve as a guiding light for you in times like this.

5. Start Rebuilding Confidence

More than ever, now is the time to start rebuilding your confidence level. Don't allow negative thoughts to get through to your head. Indulge in good, healthy activities and always protect your mind.

Gradually, you will regain your confidence and put this unpleasant phase behind you for good.

How to Build Self-Esteem after an Addiction

1. Write out Affirmations

Again, affirmations are very useful in helping you rebuild your self-esteem. Tell yourself how proud you are of all you have accomplished, and continue to speak positive words to yourself so you are encouraged to do even better.

You can write out your affirmations and place them close to where you can read them out easily every day.

2. Forgive Yourself

People who have struggled with addiction are plagued with self-blame and guilt-trip themselves, thus making it difficult for them to forgive their errors. Now isn't the time to beat yourself up over what happened in the past.

Acknowledge that what you did was wrong and then

move on from the issue by committing to doing things differently. Your past failures should not define your present.

3. Accept Compliments

When a person suffers from low self-esteem, they will be very quick to dismiss a tribute, but now that you are trying to rebuild your self-esteem, accept compliments graciously.

Smile at the person giving the compliment and ensure that you also say something nice to him/her. Accepting compliments is an easy way of bringing a lot of good into your life.

4. Do Something Kind Every Day

Kindness is therapeutic; you can increase the appreciation that others express toward you by being kind to them. Now, consideration doesn't have to be something grand or huge. By doing straightforward things, you can make someone else feel good, thus putting a smile on your own face.

You can also volunteer to help others in need as a way of rebuilding your self-esteem. If you are kind, the universe and other people will be kind to you as well.

5. Make the Necessary Changes

As you do something kind, be mindful of the fact that you will have to start making meaningful changes in your lifestyle immediately. First, you should avoid the places you used to go that weren't good for you.

You know the peculiarities of your addiction so try to put a stop to everything that will lead you back to where you were before now.

6. Get Rid of Addictive Materials

As you make the necessary changes, you should also get free of all addictive substances that will take you back to the life you are trying to escape. So videotapes, credit cards, drugs, etc. that are unhealthy for you should be thrown away.

With the addictive materials out of the way, you will be able to create an enabling environment for your new lifestyle to blossom. Go through your items and remove all traces of materials that will take you back.

7. Speak to a Therapist

A therapist is always a good idea, especially when you need to get out of severe addiction. A therapist is a third-party who will be objective in their analysis of your situation. Be open to listening and gaining insight into how you can get out of addiction.

8. Take Baby Steps

You won't get out of the habit in a flash so be ready to start by taking baby steps. Remember that it took you a while to get here, so it will take a while to get out of it as well.

Everything you decide to do to change must be handled with care; if you try to rush the process of getting out of addiction, you will fall right back into it. So, exercise patience by taking baby steps.

9. Be Patient with the Process

The fact that you have decided to change doesn't mean it is going to happen all at once. There is a process, and you must be patient with it; your ability to stay patient through it all will determine how far you go with the change.

There will be times when it seems like you might relapse; hold on tight and believe the best about yourself.

10. Love is All That Matters

When you love yourself enough, you will surely want to protect yourself from anything that is harmful to your mental, emotional, and psychological space. After getting over an addiction, what you should do is fill your mind with self-love.

Love yourself and appreciate life; it is the only way you can solidify all you have learned here. With love, you can overcome every obstacle that comes your way. Remember also to love others; it is your way of extending a hand of kindness to them.

Your life can be so much better despite addiction, but you must be willing to put up a fight for what you want. If you are not doing anything to kick the addiction out, you will continue to wallow in it.

The message of this chapter is two-fold:

1. If you are at a shallow place in your life right now, do not turn to addiction.
2. If you were able to get out of the habit, rebuild your self-esteem and maintain a clean slate with life afterward.

If you can internalize both messages, you will be on your way to a better life, free from addiction and the problems it presents. We have been going on and on about you for a while now. It is time to consider the relationships you have with other people and how they shape your self-esteem. Head over to the next chapter and read through the ideas you will find there.

Chapter Twelve

How do you treat others?

They say the way you treat others is a reflection of who you are. People with low self-esteem often treat others around them poorly because they are unhappy with themselves. So if you are going to enjoy high self-esteem, you will have to seek out ways of ensuring that you treat people well.

As simple as the opening paragraph is, so many people still fall victim to the trap of being nasty to others such that at the end of the day, they are alone because no one wants to be friends with people who aren't nice.

Well, when you stay alone long enough, you start to feel isolated, and this affects the quality of the relationships you enjoy with others. Loneliness is a breeding ground for very low self-esteem, and just like that, you find yourself having problems.

As a man who is keen on becoming an Alpha male, it is crucial that you treat others around you the same way you will want to be treated. This is a trait those with high self-esteem portray; they view everyone as equal and try to leave a lasting impression on the minds of others.

So at the end of the day, people who are friendly, kind, and giving to others can build a support system for themselves. They hear a lot of kind words as well and have a rich deposit of self-confidence.

I want you to take some time to ask yourself this all-important question; do I treat other people well? Am I a kind person? Do people leave me feeling inspired? Or am I rude and abusive? A portion of the Holy book that Christians read states that "Out of the abundance of the heart, the mouth speaks." You will only say to others what you've got on the onside.

If you are filled with a lot of hate, anger, and bitterness, you will never be kind to others, and this will gradually erode you of whatever self-esteem you've got left. This chapter isn't about you (we have been going on and on about you since we started). This chapter tries to strike a balance between what you can do to improve your self-esteem and your connections with other people.

When it comes to treating other people well, you must be deliberate about it. Being intentional with the relationships you build will cause you to appreciate the link you've got with yourself, as well. We are going to get right to the tips you can implement that will help you treat other people well enough to give your self-esteem the boost it deserves.

How to Treat Other People Well for High Self-Esteem

Be Conscious of Others

As a person who is trying to build high self-esteem, you must become aware of others. You are not an island on your own; you coexist with people around you. As such, it is essential you take into consideration their likes, dislikes, and everything else that is important to them.

When you become conscious of others, you will also discover ways through which you can be useful to them.

Start with the people around you; your home offices, out on the streets, etc., reach out to someone with a smile and make a difference just by being aware of the people around you.

1. Random Acts of Kindness

Random acts of kindness refer to the process of being friendly and kind-hearted towards people you don't even know. You could pay for a stranger's transport fare or provide food and shelter for orphans.

Only a person who is satisfied and happy with his own life will attempt helping people he doesn't know. So, you get to see the connection between being kind and self-esteem.

Random acts of kindness can also take the form of doing nice things for those you love unexpectedly. How about showing up at your friend's house with pastries and cookies on Christmas morning? You can be the most beautiful, self-accepting person ever; all you must do is start being kind to others one person at a time.

2. Listen More Than You Speak

If you pay attention to what people are saying more than you talk to them, you will discover new things about them. The person who listens receives information that is instrumental in helping him make a difference in the life of another person.

Now that you have started building self-esteem, you must become consumed with the idea of giving more of yourself in service to others. Being a good listener will help you live a very impactful life; it is a testament to how far you have come in developing your self-esteem.

3. Show Respect to All

One of the best ways to show people you care is by being

respectful to them. There is a famous saying that respect is reciprocal; and this is so true. People will only show you respect when they perceive that you are respectful to them, as well.

Show respect by honouring other people's decisions. Try not to force your ideas on others and appreciate the efforts they make every day to live well. Little words such as "Thank you," "I am sorry," or "Good morning," go a very long way showing how respectful you are toward others.

4. Accept People for Who They Are

Instead of trying to change others and make them into what you've envisaged in your head, try to be accommodating and accept them for who they are.

Everyone won't be the same, we all won't like or want the same things - and that is okay. When you meet someone who loves what you like, great! However, when you come across a person who is entirely different from you in all aspects, learn to tolerate them and work with them just as they are. Accepting people for who they are is a sign of high self-esteem.

5. Follow the Golden Rule

What does the "golden control" state? "Do to others as

you would want them to do to you". Whatever you want everyone else to do to you, start doing it to other people as well.

If you want people to smile at you, smile more often, and if you want people to share with you, go right ahead and share with others, too. If you are committed to the happiness of others, someone else or a group of people will also be committed to your happiness.

Write the golden rule plainly so you can see it and scan it. It will serve as a constant reminder that you have an obligation towards others that must be fulfilled.

6. Don't Pull People Down

This is so important! In a bid to rise to the top, too many people try to pull others down. Your light will not shine more brightly because someone else's view is dim.

Remember that we rise by lifting others.

More so, you will be affecting the self-esteem of the person you are pulling down, so it will be a case of hurting someone with something you are trying to avoid.

When you make it your lifelong mission to help everyone you meet, you won't have to think about pulling someone else down so you can rise.

7. Don't Look Down on Anyone

You may not be on the same level as everyone else, but it isn't a reason for you to look down on those who are not on the high level you perceive yourself to be on.

In the next chapter you will read about humility, and you will discover the reason why it is so essential for you to consider everyone as being equal.

The moment you start to look down on others, your self-esteem begins to diminish. Preserve all you have worked so hard for by treating everyone with fairness, dignity, respect, and love.

8. Be Gracious to All

When we speak of being polite, we refer to being incredibly kind, merciful, and compassionate towards other. A lot of people do not know how to be courteous, so they skip this step. But this one is important.

It is good to be kind, but it is better to be gracious. Being kind is something you do while being conscious; you plan for it, and it happens as you have envisioned.

Being gracious is something you do even when you don't feel like it. You go out of your way to make things happen for other people, and that is one of the hallmarks of being a man with high self-esteem.

9. Appreciate Those Who Support You

There will always be those who are your support system in life; these people cheer you on and are huge pillars you can lean on at any time. As such, you should celebrate them by showing appreciation for all they've done for you.

According to a recent study, people who do not express gratitude to those who have done well for them suffer from very low self-esteem. You are different, so it is essential that you appreciate those who hold your hand through the crises and problems you face in life.

If treating people nicely is a prerequisite for you to enjoy the best of self-esteem, then I suggest that you take it seriously. You will only feel as good as you make others feel. When people speak of how well you treat them, it is an opportunity for you to pat yourself on the back.

Now, the fact that you are determined to help others and treat them well doesn't mean everyone will be helpful to you, as well. Come on, it is a cold world after all. But regardless of how you are treated, you must insist on taking this path and not looking back.

You shouldn't be kind to others because they are helpful to you; be generous because it is your nature to be that way. People with very high self-esteem go out of their way to make things happen for others. Another trait of a person with high self-esteem is humility; the next chapter does justice to this feature.

Chapter Thirteen

Humility is a Tool

We have been on such a fantastic ride from the very first chapter until now, and it gets better and better with each section. Now we are going to consider a vital tool needed in giving your self-esteem a significant boost; and that tool is Humility.

Everyone wants to be associated with humble people who make them feel special. Come on, ordinary people are just the best, aren't they? So why not be the humble person who makes other people feel excited? It is quite rare to find people with very high self-esteem who are rude and proud.

Good self-esteem is a product of a mind that has accepted all of its flaws and imperfections and still thinks he is fantastic. There is a feeling of humility that comes with being able to say, "Oh, I know I am not perfect, but I am on my way to greater things."

If you are always humble, you will not struggle with

maintaining high self-esteem; it will become a lifestyle for you. But humility must be practiced; it must be groomed and nurtured over time for it to be sustained. More importantly, as a humble person, you will be able to influence others as well.

As opposed to popular opinion, humility is not a sign of low self-esteem. People can be very humble yet exhibit a high sense of appreciation for who they are and the journey they have been on.

I want you to think about humility and self-esteem from two perspectives. First, you can utilize humility as a tool to build self-esteem, and second, you can use it to gain power over people.

So, what you should be concerned with in this chapter is how to use humility as a tool for the advancement of your self-esteem. You must have observed that almost every section in this book contains steps, tips, and ideas. Well, the reason for the levels is for you to have something you can hold on to even after reading the book.

I can come here and write an epistle. I can go on and on about how you can be humble. But, if I don't show you the steps to take, it will all be a waste of time. So once again, I request your indulgence as you read through steps you can take toward using humility to build higher self-esteem.

With these steps, you will be required to take action immediately as you learn them. After every tip, there is an accountability step that ensures you utilize the step.

How to Build Higher Self-Esteem through Humility

1. Be Available for People

Humility is about putting yourself aside for others, sometimes. The best way to show that you care for someone is by being available for them.

Sometimes we pride ourselves in being so busy that we forget the importance of being a pillar of strength someone can lean on in difficult times. It takes a person with healthy self-esteem to be there for someone else despite having their challenges.

Your friends and family members, as well as strangers, should say that you are a reliable person - someone they can count on at any time.

Accountability Task: Go through your messages and chats with friends, discover who is experiencing a tough time right now, and create time in your schedule to be there for them.

When you show up for that person, don't make the entire situation about you; the more you do this for others, the better you will feel about yourself.

2. Avoid Baseless Arguments

Arguments are good. In fact, most intellectual conversations stem from arguments. But, baseless arguments are a complete waste of time. Whenever you find yourself in a gathering where people shout and scream to prove their point, get out of there.

Humility is all about positivity. If you are going to have a conversation with someone that isn't positive, then you must start to consider bringing that conversation to an end.

Baseless arguments will also make you think less of yourself, especially when you are struggling with the idea of building a very firm, strong self-esteem. Be smart enough to know when to let go of a discussion.

Accountability Task: The next time you go out with friends and colleagues, be mindful of the kind of conversations you engage in with them. Once the discussion starts to go south, that is the signal for you to take your leave.

3. Admit when You are Wrong

When you meet a person who is unable to admit their wrongs, you have just reached a proud person. We haven't come this far to be proud now, have we? So, you are going to kick that feeling out by admitting to your wrongs.

People with low self-esteem will always want to insist on being right, regardless of how glaring their fault is. Be a noble person by accepting your wrongs and doing your best to become a better person.

Accountability Task: The next time you do something wrong, admit to it and learn your lesson. If you weren't aware that you made a wrong move, when others point it out to you, try not to be defensive. Life is not about being right all the time; it is about growing and learning.

4. Be a Cheerleader

We love cheerleaders because they add colour and fun to the game. But in life, cheerleaders do more than that. Cheerleaders in real life don't get to wear costumes; they are our most significant support systems which will take our hands when we are faced with a challenge and help us walk through it with confidence.

The point is this; you have to be a cheerleader to someone else. Now the person might be a subordinate, but they will be grateful for the help you render. Cheer your partners on; clap and celebrate with your friends when they reach a milestone.

With cheerleading in life, it isn't about who is

winning; it is all about being there for anyone who wins.

Accountability task: You have got to have someone you cheer on currently. Look within your inner circle and search for that person who is embarking on a project and needs a little help. Remember that you reflect how you make people feel.

5. Help Others Become Better

As you cheer others on, make sure you are taking steps toward making them feel better, as well. It is so easy for us to become self-absorbed and think about ourselves. After all, we are all that matters right? But this shouldn't be the case.

Your ability to reach out to someone with an idea or skill that will help them is one of the hallmarks of humility. People continually seek better ways of doing things through collaborations, so who are you working with now? How can you make that best friend of yours extremely good at what they do?

By always thinking about others, you will be helping yourself, as well.

Accountability Task: Think about something you can do for someone that will add value to their experience. It doesn't have to be something big; most times the smallest gestures mean the most to others.

6. Give People Credit

In a bid to be harsh, we often withhold credit when it is due for others, and this is wrong. If you are a leader in your sector, it is okay for you to be stern when you need to be - but also give credit to others when it is due.

How would you feel knowing that you have done a great job and your boss doesn't even acknowledge it? Oh, I bet you would feel so terrible that it might affect your self-esteem.

If you don't want to work with people who have low self-esteem, make sure you give them credit when it is due. Also, if you're going to enjoy very high self-esteem continually, you must be kind to other people. It is a way of extending kindness to yourself, as well.

Accountability Task: Reward excellence the next time someone does something remarkable for you.

7. Don't Compare People

It can all be fun and games when you compare Mr. A with Mr. B, but trust me when I say it isn't right. The art of putting two people side by side doesn't showcase humility. Nor does it make you a better person.

Always remember that people are different. Your ability to accept them for who they are is what makes you stand out and aids in maintaining better relationships with others.

Be the man who walks into a room and can reach out to everyone, regardless of their flaws. Be a friend to all and a man of great character; humility will make you stand out.

Accountability Task: Appreciate the goodness in other people by looking out for their great traits and not their flaws. Let each one you know be an original and not a duplicate of another person. Be kind with your words and avoid the pitfalls of comparison.

8. Be Teachable

Have you observed that people who are not teachable are often very proud? Oh yes, they are! When a person becomes unteachable, they also find it difficult to build good self-esteem. You must make up your mind to be someone who can make changes at any time.

By being teachable, we are referring to the art of being an avid learner who has an open mind toward life. You are not stereotyped; neither should you insist on having your way all the time.

A person with high self-esteem realizes that they can learn from other people in the same way they can teach others.

Accountability Task: Make up your mind to learn something new. Seek out someone who can teach you, and regardless of the person's social status, be open to learning and adding more to your knowledge.

9. Volunteer

It is always a good time to give to others. Therefore, volunteering is crucial. You can show how humble you are by reaching out to people you don't know and people who may never have enough to pay you back.

There are multiple opportunities through which you can volunteer: homeless shelters, orphanages, old people's homes, etc. Seek out the organization you like and do something special for them.

You will be amazed at how great you feel every time you volunteer to help others. This process also aids in building better self-esteem; so keep at it for the long haul.

Accountability task: Make a list of all the non-profit organizations you know. From that list, create a plan that entails you paying a visit to one of the groups at least once a month. Ensure that you stick to your plans monthly, weekly or yearly (it depends on what works best for you).

Humility is not just about being modest; it is all about being able to handle yourself in a classy way and still make an impact on the lives of others. What we have achieved with this chapter is teaching you some of the most effective steps you can take toward building self-esteem through a humble mindset.

As we wrap up this chapter, please be reminded that HUMILITY IS POWER UNDER CONTROL.

You've got all the power, yet you can put others first; that is what humility is all about. We spoke briefly about falling in love with yourself a while back; let's take it a step further as we analyse more about that concept in the next chapter.

Chapter Fourteen

Falling in Love with Yourself

We spoke about this briefly in the previous section, but it is just too important to only get a brief mention. Self-esteem is all about love! We cannot talk about building self-esteem without talking about how much we should love ourselves and others.

Love is a significant ingredient needed to build up one's self-esteem and sustain it long term (we will consider the steps you should take toward sustainability in the last chapter, look forward to reading that).

So, for you to grow and improve your self-esteem, you have to first love yourself. The extent to which you love yourself determines how you will love others, as well. You cannot give what you don't have. As such, you can only express love to people from the abundance of love you feel for yourself.

How well you love yourself will also go a long way in showing how patient you will be with others. A person who loves themselves will do everything within their power to be happy! Happy people are individuals with amazing self-esteem; they are so satisfied with their lives that they are not willing to allow negative feelings into their minds.

How do you know you love yourself? What are the indicators that show how much you appreciate who you are? If you were going to recommend yourself as a friend to someone, would you say you are a great person? Questions like these should put a lot of things into perspective for you.

Love is about acceptance.

Love is about embracing all of who you are.

Love is the feeling of content

Love is being committed to one's happiness.

Love is patient.

Love is about kindness.

Love is high self-esteem.

If you are not sure about the love you have for yourself, I want you to carry out a brief exercise before we go on. Get your journal and write down ten things you love about yourself. The ten things can cut across skills, abilities, and behavioural patterns.

After writing, read these traits out loud to yourself and reaffirm that you have got the present in your life for good. If you are honest with yourself, you will realize that indeed there is so much about you that is good and worthy of celebration.

With self-love, you don't have to wait for someone else to tell you how special you are. Self-love is like a spring that bursts forth from within you and sprinkles life, hope, and more love into every area of your life. You have to turn on the faucet of this spring by first recognizing all the great qualities you've got on the inside.

No one is a complete flop; there may be a time when it seems like you don't have it all together, but if you embrace your truth, you will realize that you are a superstar who has a few bumps once in a while.

In this chapter, you are going to come across the top ten principles of self-love and discover how you can use these principles in your own life. The key to getting the best out of these steps is simple; READ, UNDERSTAND, ACT, AND DON'T STOP ACTING! I can't wait for us to get to the chapter on sustenance, so let's wrap this up quickly because the last section is already upon us.

Principles of Self-love for Better Self-Esteem

1. The Law of Self-Compassion

Self-love can only become fully manifested when you are compassionate toward yourself. This principle is akin to being conscious of what your weaknesses are and still loving who you are regardless.

You can practice compassion through patience; when you fall off the path you have crafted for yourself, pick yourself up and move on purposefully. Compassionate people are known to be kind, as well. It is safe to say that this principle urges you to be kind.

Whenever you feel tempted to be hard on yourself, remember that you are on this journey of self-love and it is imperative to show compassion toward yourself.

2. The Principle of Being Responsible

Self-love will not be easily accomplished when you are irresponsible with your life. A responsible person shows that they have regard for their life, so they make very wise choices that guide them through their journey.

Being responsible isn't a trait you can negotiate or do without. You have got to show an excellent example by examining the life choices you make and ensuring that these choices align with the greater vision you have for your life.

Don't do things that hurt yourself; self-love is tender and gentle. Be committed to living responsibly today as you take time off daily to analyse the choices you make and how they affect you long term.

3. The Principle of Being Non-Judgemental of Yourself

In a bid to be excellent, you will want to be highly critical, and this will lead to being judgemental. Love doesn't pass judgment even in worst-case scenarios. Avoid being too hard on yourself and trust that you are on the right path regardless of the challenges you face.

Being non-judgemental also pushes you to accept yourself, know your strengths, and strategize on how to work on your weaknesses. Even when you are angered by your actions and inactions, don't judge yourself.

Always remember that you are the captain of this ship and you must be in charge, leading with love and self-acceptance.

4. The Principle of Patience

We cannot talk about self-love without patience. Some people give up on themselves because they aren't patient enough to see all their efforts come to fruition. Being patient doesn't mean you tolerate bad behaviour, it means you get to appreciate where you are now while hoping for the best to come.

Love and patience go together; you cannot love without being patient, and you cannot be patient if you don't love. As you focus on building high self-esteem, be determined to be patient with yourself on this journey and take into consideration the areas you can improve upon.

5. The Principle of Quiet Acceptance

This principle speaks of a person accepting themselves as they are. It is often easy to take yourself for granted, especially when you feel like you can be more. Love will make you admit who you are because love is about faith.

Don't wait for someone else to give you approval or offer you a commendation for being a good person. Remember that this journey is all about your personality, so you've got to take responsibility for it.

When you come to a place of acceptance, you also let go of fear. You investigate the future with hope knowing that you are enough.

6. The Principle of Faith in the Unknown

The reason some people start to feel a sense of low self-esteem is that they are sceptical about the future. So, they wake up every day in panic mode, thinking about how their tomorrow will turn out and how they will get the best out of their day.

Well, if you continue to be apprehensive about the future, you will probably never learn to love yourself. It is okay to wonder what will happen next, but it is not alright for you to WORRY about it.

Love is about embracing today and having faith in a future that may be unknown. By being sceptical, you may draw yourself back into the shell of low self-esteem. So be bold about tomorrow, because love conquers all things - even the future.

7. The Principle of Being Authentic

Through it all, remember that you are an original and not a copy of someone else. You must follow through with the policy of being genuine and real.

Love is about embracing all of you and being real about it. The best way to love anyone is to accept them for who they are; but the best way to enjoy yourself is by being authentic with your story.

Don't try to be like someone else; don't try to take

snippets of another man's life and add to yours. You are already on your way to a more magnificent journey of self-esteem, so don't ruin it by being unsure of who you are.

8. The Principle of Love and Health

Self-love will not work out for anyone who isn't mindful of health. Come on, would you be reading this book if you were unhealthy? Would you be able to implement all these principles if you were in the hospital?

They say, "Health is wealth," but I say health is EVERYTHING!

The ideas behind self-love will only be what they are – ideas. Until you start working on them from a position of good health, you will not enjoy the process. To adhere to this principle, make sure you are full of health enough to love yourself unconditionally.

9. The Principle of Positive Self-Talk

Most of the activities you will be required to do concerning self-love have to do with your ability to speak to yourself. Remember that you are on this journey for the long haul; no one else will make you love yourself.

You are at the centre of this process and whatever you say or believe about yourself is what will hold sway in your life. You are building positive self-esteem. As such, you will have to reaffirm all the good you see in yourself.

10. The Principle of Peace with Self

Above all, be at peace with yourself. Where there is love, greater peace reigns supreme. If you are always having internal conflict, negative emotions, and a lack of confidence, you will find it difficult to love yourself.

This last principle is so important because there are a lot of people who are unable to love themselves because they don't feel at peace with who they are. Such people will have to get rid of the conflict and settle for a life of peace where love can thrive.

Life can be very dynamic. Some things may happen and spring up on you causing you to lose your peace, but you must be resolute in your determination to love yourself and enjoy peace even as you build higher self-esteem.

These principles will work best when you are deliberate about utilizing them. I always urge readers to look beyond the words on the written page. Instead, readers should think about how these words will come alive through actionable steps.

If you have already practised some of these principles,

strengthen your resolve to do more with them. If you haven't worked on any of them yet, be determined to act today. You will be amazed at the extent of growth and improvement you make with your self-esteem.

Finally, we are getting to the very last chapter. I am so excited because it is a culmination of all we have learned from the beginning until now. You already know that this last chapter deals with the concept of sustenance, so let's get right to it.

Chapter Fifteen

The Art of Sustaining Self-Esteem

Well, we are in the last part of our journey, and I believe it has been as rewarding an experience for you as it has been for me. When we started, you had a lot of questions, and as we made progress, you discovered the answers you sought. Good self-esteem is a prerequisite for success in life, and knowing how to build it is a skill that is necessary for growth.

With every good thing that has a beginning, there is also an end. The end of this journey is here, but it is the start of greater things to come, because unlike when we started, you are now equipped with information that will upgrade your life for good.

Self-esteem is not built by just reading a book. Oh, if that was the pathway, by now there would be fewer people with low self-esteem, right? However, a man has got to do more than just read; he must take action, try, fail, and try again until he perfects the process.

So, with all you have read thus far, try not to get it right all at once. It takes time to build solid self-esteem, and if you put in the work, you will reap the rewards of such an effort. This chapter aims to show you ways through which you can SUSTAIN all you have read up to this point.

Let's talk about sustenance for a while, shall we?

When a person learns how to do something, they gain a skill or new ability. If the person exercises that ability for a while, they will become very good at it. But if they are unable to maintain the pace with which to do it repeatedly, they will gradually lose that skill without even knowing it.

Sustainability is about doing something long enough that it becomes a part of you. It is like maintaining a new car; you drive it for a while and then once in a while you take it to the mechanic for regular checks. Now, if you fail to carry out those regular checks, the car will break down someday, and then you will spend more fixing it.

Now you know all about how to build self-esteem and what you must do to make it a vital part of your life. But how do you sustain all you learned now? How can you ensure that the lessons you've gained remain with you for a long time? How do you maintain the standard you've built? The answers to the questions above lie within the steps you can take below.

How to Sustain a Very High Self-Esteem

1. Always Do the Best You Can

One way of sustaining all you have learned is by striving to do your best. With whatever lesson you want to implement, put in the best effort, give your all, and avoid being mediocre.

When you are committed to doing your best, you will enjoy higher self-esteem. There will be a feeling of satisfaction within you knowing that you are on the right path and your efforts will be victorious.

You can be the best all the time!

2. Enjoy Positive Relationships

High self-esteem can be sustained when you nurture positive relationships. You will become a product of the people you hang out with the most. So, if you are always around those who bring down your self-esteem with hurtful words, it is time to re-evaluate your relationships.

At this point, you are looking at creating new bonds with people who have great personality traits. The more time you spend with great people, the better your chances of improving your self-esteem. Positive relationships are complementary, so ensure that you also add value to the people you spend time with. Give more to get more.

3. Be Happy Every Day

Happiness happens from a place of content satisfaction. For you to sustain your self-esteem goals, you must ensure that you are committed to your happiness.

Every day, wake up with a smile on your face knowing that you can be the happiest human being in the world. As you build self-esteem, you will observe that you are always pleased and content with yourself.

Let happiness lead you to a life of fulfilment and ever-growing self-esteem.

4. Take on the Gratitude Challenge

The gratitude challenge requires you to take account of everything you are grateful for on your journey. This is one very impactful way of sustaining your self-esteem. Look around you right now; there is so much to be thankful for. If you are not conscious of this, you will live a miserable life.

Practise the gratitude challenge every day by counting your blessings and giving your self-esteem the daily boost it requires. One of the ways to implement the gratitude challenge is by keeping a gratitude journal.

Take the journal with you everywhere you go and keep your records. At the end of the day go through all you wrote down and go to bed smiling with a heart full of joy.

5. Cultivate Healthier Habits

We dedicated a chapter to addictions and how they can ruin your self-esteem. Well, for you to sustain all you have learned, you must cultivate the right habits.

Adopt habits that are productively positive, inspiring, and cause you to focus on your goals. Read good books, join a self-esteem men's club, exercise, etc. These are some of the most productive habits you can create.

You will always be a product of the habits you build, so watch closely and pay attention to the things you often do; they will determine how far you go in building your self-esteem.

6. Do What You Love

This step should be taken seriously if you truly want to sustain all you have learned. By doing what you like, you will be positioning yourself as a man who loves himself and is passionate about living on his terms.

Do not allow anyone or any circumstances to force you into doing what you don't like or want. With firmness of heart and a resolution to do only what inspires you, your self-esteem is bound to experience a significant improvement.

Let love lead you on this path; love is the light that never misguides.

7. Forget About Perfectionism

The idea of perfectionism doesn't exist!

No one is perfect; everyone is a work in progress. So don't beat yourself up because you are not perfect. Be inspired to do your best and forget about the idea of being perfect.

There is beauty in trying to be a better person, and when you accept yourself for who you are without the pressures of wanting to be perfect, you will be able to build high self-esteem that is sturdy and inspiring to others.

8. Be Your Own Best Friend

You are all you've got at the end of the day. You have a responsibility to be your own best friend, so play that role well. Learn to advise yourself and cheer yourself on when you win. Also, learn to be your source of strength when the chips are down.

Some people who have experienced low self-esteem often say that they got to that point because no one was there for them when they needed a hand. However, think about it this way; if you were your own best friend, would you rely on someone else for support. Even if you had a perfect support system, you would still be able to handle your issues well by yourself.

9. Avoid Negative Environmental Factors

There are factors in your environment and immediate sphere of contact that conflict with your plans for improved self-esteem. Now is the time to identify those factors and avoid them altogether.

Adverse environmental factors should never be a consideration, especially if you are keen on growing on this journey. Adverse environmental factors may be in the form of neighbours who try to intimidate you with properties they've got.

Whatever type of negativity abounds in your environment, avoid it and protect your mental space from it.

10. Try Something New Often

Who doesn't love new things? Everyone does! So try them; new skills, new books, clothes, friends, experiences etc. People who suffer from low self-esteem always try to shy away from new things because they hold on to their comfort zone.

After reading this book, the only thing you should hold on to is a renewed mindset that aids the changes you want to see in your self-esteem. So be open and free; be willing to take on new adventures because life is all about learning and growing.

If you try something new and you don't like it, you will learn a lesson - but never stop trying!

11. Remember Why You Need Good Self-Esteem

Always remind yourself why you are embarking on this journey. Sometimes you need to be told, so you maintain focus and go ahead with your plans.

When it seems like you are going off course, remind yourself of the values you have and pursue your goals with vigour and focus. It will not always be a pleasant journey, and things will not always go as planned, but one thing is sure in the end, your self-esteem will not remain at the same level.

Consciously and deliberately work on yourself as you aspire to build unshakeable self-esteem.

12. Come Back to the Lessons in This Book

At every turn on this adventure, make sure you come back to the experiences in this book. You shouldn't read through and forget everything you've learned. If you have an issue with any area we have treated in previous chapters, go back to the section to remind yourself of the solutions and steps that were given.

This book is your ultimate guide and best friend; read, read again, and share the lessons with other people. You will be building a network of people that have high self-esteem just like you.

13. Trust Your Decisions

On the path of sustainability, you will be required to make a lot of choices, and it is imperative that you trust the decisions you make. A man who is undecided will be confused - and being confused is a feature of low self-esteem.

If you have trained your mind to recognise and appreciate the best of life, you will always arrive at a favourable conclusion when making decisions. If you don't trust yourself enough, you may have to lean on other people's opinions. And you know what they say about the views of others - they just may not fit with yours.

14. Don't Go Back to Your Shell

Regardless of what happens to you on this journey, never go back to the shell of low self-esteem. Fight off the desire to go back at all costs and maintain the same consistency you've created with your self-esteem.

At some point, you may feel the urge to go back because you are pressured, but if you resist it with great attributes and a renewed mindset to keep up with the journey, you will succeed.

The shell you think you can go back to is not the solution; it is a trap that will take you back to what you should be running from.

15. Create a Pattern

Patterns are like habits - but you can be way more consistent with them. So, with models, you must consider some of the good things you can do that will enhance your self-esteem and be committed to doing them REGULARLY.

With patterns, you can imbibe the right activities and traits all at once. You will also be able to inspire someone else to develop their self-esteem as you share your story.

So, when you wake up at the same time of the day and do the same exciting things that make you happy, you can watch your self-esteem receive a significant boost.

Knowledge isn't power; it is the APPLICATION of knowledge that is power. Knowing what to do doesn't cause any change within you; it is doing it and succeeding at it that transforms your life.

So, with all you have learned now, ensure that you are not only building self-esteem but also sustaining it.

There is one more section you should read; it is the concluding section that ultimately brings the book to an end. There is a special message in that chapter for you, hurry over there now and get started.

Conclusion

What an incredible journey we have had, and it all comes to an end right here. From gaining information on the meaning of self-esteem to learning about self-acceptance and other vital life processes needed to boost your self-esteem.

What we have achieved together with this book will go a long way in helping you build higher self-esteem. It also positions you as an Alpha-male in whatever industry or environment you find yourself. The chapters you read through contain lessons that will be extremely useful to you long term.

So, what is the special message I've got for you in this concluding section? It is a message about the power of being proactive. There are millions of men out there who can relate to everything they have read in this book, yet they lack self-esteem.

The reason for their inability to continue with all they've learned is because they are not proactive enough. In life, we've got two kinds of people; the PROACTIVE and the REACTIVE. The proactive individuals take steps to get what they want, and they succeed.

The reactive ones, on the other hand, wait for

situations to happen to them. As such, they end up not being able to achieve anything long term. You should aspire to become a proactive person who can bring the words in this book to life through consistent and sustainable action-plans.

People who lead with great self-esteem are also proactive enough to reach out to others who haven't attained such heights in life. As you help others improve how they feel about themselves, you will be able to solidify all you've gained, as well.

The previous chapter elucidated on the art of sustainability; you were given some steps on how you can sustain all you've learned. From time to time, go back to that chapter and remind yourself what you can do to maintain the self-confidence you've gained.

The book comes to an end here but guess what? It is the start of a brand-new journey for you. Look ahead with faith, give your confidence a significant boost, and don't stop improving on yourself.

I look forward to reading your testimonials as you proactively apply the tips you've been given.

Remember that all good things take time, but with determination and a commitment to excellence, you will stand out from the crowd. Thank you for being such a good sport and sticking it out with me through this book. It is time for you to go forth and win with the most positive attitude towards life and unshakeable self-esteem.

Best wishes to you now and always!!

www.ingramcontent.com/pod-product-compliance
Lightning Source LLC
Chambersburg PA
CBHW071502080526
44587CB00014B/2186